THE BUSINESS OF FRIENDSHIP

SHASTA NELSON

THE BUSINESS OF FRIENDSHIP

Making the Most of
Our Relationships Where
We Spend Most of Our Time

HarperCollins Leadership
An Imprint of HarperCollins

Published by HarperCollins Leadership, an imprint of HarperCollins Focus LLC.

Book design by Aubrey Khan, Neuwirth & Associates.

ISBN 978-1-4002-1697-0 (eBook)
ISBN 978-1-4002-1696-3 (HC)
ISBN 978-1-4002-1699-4 (TP)

Library of Congress Control Number: 2020938776

To Greg, my husband, and also my favorite coworker.
Office holiday parties with you are the best!

And for Naomi, Myles, Edda, Asa, Dante, Lily, and Lucy—the little people in my heart: it is my hope that when you one day contribute to our workforce, no matter what you do, you thoroughly enjoy those who do it with you.

Contents

Research and References ix

Introduction: Why We Need This Book xi

PART 1

Why Relationships Matter at Work

1 How We Benefit from Friendships at Work 3

2 How Our Company Benefits from Our Friendships at Work 21

PART 2

What Makes All Relationships Actually Work?

3 What Is a Friendship? 35
The Three Relationship Requirements

4 How Friendships Are Developed 47
The Frientimacy Triangle

5 How to Develop Relationships at Work That Are Positive 63

6 How to Develop Relationships at Work That Are Consistent 81

✓ INCLUDING: how to feel close when working remotely, on global teams, or alone

7 How to Develop Relationships at Work That Are Vulnerable 105

PART 3

How to Make Relationships Work Better for Us

8 Healthy Goals and Expectations for Relationships at Work 127
Do We Have to be Friends With Everyone?

9 Reducing the Impact of "Toxic" Coworkers 139
Two Ways to Respond to Unhealthy Relationships

10 Increasing Belonging When We Feel Left Out 155
How to Respond to Cliques and Other Best Friends

✓ INCLUDING: how to minimize gossip on our team

11 Fear of Favoritism, or Does It Have to Be Lonely at the Top? 169
How to Support Our Leaders Having Friends

12 Becoming Best Friends at Work 183
How to Develop Appropriate Friendships That Benefit the Team

✓ INCLUDING: how to navigate the workplace when we're not getting along

✓ INCLUDING: how to protect our relationships from unwanted romantic bonding

In Closing 201

About Free Bonus Chapter 203

Advice for Managers 205

Resources and Ideas for Friendships at Work 211

Notes 213

Research and References

This book stands on the shoulders of some amazing researchers who have long been studying relationships, business, culture, and health in their respective fields. I do my best to footnote every study I quote in the back of this book and am in deep gratitude for their curiosity in asking big questions, their bravery for pursuing the answers, and their wisdom in their reporting. (The biggest of thanks for Kiran Adcock for compiling all those citations!)

While my expertise runs deep in friendship research and application, having written two other books on the subject, my foray into the world of business will forever be indebted to the visionary leaders who started inviting me to speak to their organizations, facilitate their team off-site meetings, and consult their managers. As promised, your names and organizations do not show up in this book, but your wisdom is loud and clear, and your stories and examples are everywhere. And even more of you took your teams through my *Healthy Team Relationship Assessment*, which not only gave you an accessible report on the health of the relationships within your team, but that collective data continues to reveal so much about the trends, tendencies, and needs we all face in our organizational culture.

Additionally, I facilitated my own *Friendships in the Workplace Survey* via social media, in which 550 respondents answered almost thirty questions about their opinions and experiences of relationships at work. These responses were invaluable, not only for the snapshot they provide of what many of us are feeling (which I'll be showing in graphs throughout this book), but the results ended up reshaping part of my book outline when I saw the incredible prevalence of some questions and fears. Additionally, their open-ended comments and stories are woven throughout this book (with fictitious names) as they give significance to what is otherwise just a statistic. If you were one who took the time to fill out that survey, thank you; my trusty calculator and I poured over your answers every which way, with wholehearted earnestness, like a kid on Christmas morning.

Speaking of stories, I am grateful to a private Facebook group of volunteers, who generously shared illustrations, triggered ideas, and acted as a focus group for me throughout my writing process. Huge thanks, also, to those of you who agreed to phone interviews with me so I could add details to your stories, updates to the data, and tips for those in similar situations. In most cases I changed your names, and in some I changed some details, but you'll undoubtedly recognize your contribution.

And in informal, but never less important, ways, I share stories throughout this book that have long stayed with me from conversations with friends, coaching clients, and off-site meetings with employees.

All that to say, that while writing a book is often solitary work, the finished product was very much a community effort. (Not that any of us who value relationships are the least bit surprised!)

Introduction

Why We Need This Book

"I'm not here to make friends."

Words spoken at workplaces around the world.

For some, this oft-repeated line is used like a war cry to justify our competitive behavior, to shrug off what others think of us, or to convince ourselves why the end justifies the means. For others, we simply whisper it as our affirmation for why we're heading home instead of joining our coworkers for a round of drinks; we assure ourselves that it's best to keep a clear line between our professional and personal lives.

So many of us—employees and managers alike—still have serious doubts when it comes to making friends at work. When I wrote my other two books—one on making new friends as an adult and the other on how to deepen our friendships—no one challenged me as to whether those were appropriate topics. But upon moving those very-needed friendships to our workplaces where we spend most of our time? Almost 30 percent of us aren't so sure.

It is appropriate to have a best friend at work.[1]				
Definitely True	*Probably True*	*I Don't Know*	*Probably False*	*Definitely False*
36%	35%	15%	11%	3%

Now, obviously, the good news is that the remaining 70 percent of us are more or less on board with the idea of close friendships at work. And, in fact, if we have a best friend at work now, we're closer to 90 percent convinced it's a good thing.

With best friend: It is appropriate to have a best friend at work.				
Definitely True	*Probably True*	*I Don't Know*	*Probably False*	*Definitely False*
64%	26%	5%	3%	2%

No best friend: It is appropriate to have a best friend at work.				
Definitely True	*Probably True*	*I Don't Know*	*Probably False*	*Definitely False*
20%	36%	22%	16%	6%

Put a different way, we are three times more likely to think it's appropriate to have a best friend *if* we are experiencing the benefits of one, and conversely, we're three times more likely to say it's definitely inappropriate if we don't have one.

Unfortunately, too many of us don't have one. One of the largest workplace studies to date shows 42 percent of us don't have one.[2] By my survey, the number was even higher with 53 percent of us not thinking we do.

Currently, I have at least one best friend at work.				
Definitely True	*Probably True*	*I Don't Know*	*Probably False*	*Definitely False*
23%	17%	7%	19%	34%

And most of us wish we did.

I wish I had a best friend at work.				
Definitely True	*Probably True*	*I Don't Know*	*Probably False*	*Definitely False*
29%	31%	15%	13%	12%

Most of this book is written for the majority of us who want better friendships at work—maybe even a best friend. I'll teach you the science behind how relationships work, provide advice for navigating through some of our fears, and help set healthy expectations for the workplace.

But, before we get into the *how* for those who know they want those closer friendships, let's start with making the case for *why* we should all want more friendships at work and see if those of us who have been conditioned in the leave-your-personal-life-at-the-door philosophy might be open to the research that says otherwise.

What if these close relationships that scare us so much could actually help us be happier, healthier, and more productive at work and at home?

WHAT IF . . . FRIENDSHIPS AREN'T JUST A PERSONAL LIFE ISSUE?

The belief that "friends" are to be relegated to the "personal life" still permeates so many of our beliefs. In her book *How to Be Happy at Work,* leadership advisor Dr. Annie McKee says with the clarity that comes from a lifetime of studying teams and leaders, "One of the most pernicious myths in today's organizations is that you don't have to be friends with your coworkers. Common sense and my decades of work with people and companies show the exact opposite."[3] In fact, while too many in our world report feeling lonely, among the fortunate ones who don't, 99 percent of them report having meaningful connections at work.[4]

The truth is, my friends, that I've been out here preaching friendship for more than a decade—two books, dozens of YouTube videos, hundreds of keynotes and team off-site meetings, and hundreds of media interviews—and what I know to be true is this: our loneliness is less a personal issue that reflects on us as individuals as much as it's a systemic issue that will be solved only when we're willing to collectively and radically reorient our lives to that which really matters most to us, our relationships. Our friendships are not a "personal life" issue but a human issue that needs to be addressed in all aspects of our lives. And top of that list should be our work, where we spend so much of our lives.

Indeed, if we're coming home from our jobs lonely, it's almost impossible to make up for it in our off hours. If we relegate our friendships to our nonwork life—where we have to try to "fit them in" between exercise classes, kids, walking the dog, binge-watching our favorite show, running errands, cleaning the house, and sleeping—not only do we not have enough time to regularly clock the hours we need in order to feel close to people, but if we're coming home lonely then we also won't have the energy.

Steve, a pharmacist, articulated his experience painfully well on the *Friendships in the Workplace Survey*: "The problem with my weekends, besides the fact that I'm already starting to get depressed as Monday looms nearer, is that I'm so tired from the week that all I can do is the bare minimum with my family and chores—which means making time for friendships takes more energy than I have."

He nailed this vicious cycle on the head: if our workplace relationships drain our energy then it's more likely that we have less energy to invest in relationships outside of work, which then contributes to us feeling burned out and exhausted at work. As the authors of *The Happiness Track* say in a *Harvard Business Review* article about burnout at work: "The more people are exhausted, the lonelier they feel." Their research found that 50 percent of respondents, from a wide range of professions, are lonely and burned out at work.[5] For our sake—to feel less burned out by our work (and therefore feel more energy when we're away from work), we would be wise to foster supportive friendships at the very places where we need to protect ourselves from the effects of stress.

But our workplaces need us to have friends here too. For our health and happiness, yes; but also because the more we feel like we belong, the more loyal and engaged we are to them. And the truth is that while we may like our paycheck, job description, or even the brand where we work, it is only the people we work with who can determine whether we feel like we belong, or not.

In the first section of this book—the next two chapters—I lay out the research (and there's a lot of it) that will hopefully convince all of us, and our bosses, that friendships are not just worth it at work but are actually helpful.

WHAT IF . . . FRIENDSHIPS INCREASE PRODUCTIVITY AT WORK?

Speaking of helpful, by far the greatest fear we have about friendships at work is that they'll negatively affect our work.

Organizations like Gallup (one of the most reputable, comprehensive, and long-standing organizations to be providing organizational analytics) have been reporting the importance of having "a best friend" at work for nearly two decades. And other researchers have only piled on. There isn't a single study that shows we perform better, or are happier, without friends at work; and yet twenty years later, too many of us still pause, shake our heads a bit, and grimace when the subject comes up. It's like we don't *really* believe all the studies that show that liking whom we work with is one of the most significant predictors for our engagement, retention, inventory control, safety, and productivity.

But our fears and hesitations don't change the data. They've retested it with softer words like "good" or "close" or just "friend," but despite whether we are comfortable with it or not, it's those with "best friends" who make the best employees. As they say themselves, they "would have dropped the statement if not for one stubborn fact: It predicts performance."[6]

To be clear: they're saying that not only do friendships *not* hurt our productivity, they actually help it.

The real question we want to ask then isn't "Are work friendships good or bad?" Or even "Are they appropriate?" They are good *and* appropriate—even desirable from an organizational perspective. The better question we should be asking then is "How can we make work friendships the healthiest they can be—both for the sake of the employee and the mission of the company?"

And the answer isn't to discourage friendships but rather to teach healthy relationship skills that will benefit the entire workforce.

Because ask those same people who are uncomfortable with friendships in the workplace what they *do* want from their colleagues, and most of them would say yes to a list that looks pretty similar to what we'd expect from friends:

- Do you want to *enjoy* whom you work with?
- Do you want to feel like you can *trust* the people around you to "have your back" and *support* you when needed?
- Do you want to feel *valued* for who you are, the ideas you have, the work you do, and the way you contribute?
- Do you want to look forward to coming to work because you *feel a part* of something bigger?

What we say we want actually sounds a lot like friendship. For some reason we resist the word, even when we want the outcome.

Yes, we may not want to be best friends with everyone, but if given the choice—don't we at least want as many of the positive and rewarding aspects of friendship from as many of our coworkers, clients, and managers as possible? Absolutely.

In the second section of this book, "What Makes All Relationships Actually Work?" (Chapters 3–7), I teach all of us—whether we're overwhelmed with the responsibility to lead, manage, and create a healthy work environment for others, or completely underwhelmed by the lack of authority we have to make key workplace changes—how better relationships start with us. We don't need a budget, title, or even fun colleagues to get started. We'll define friendship and make sure we know what we're aiming toward so we can create the relationships that bring us more joy at work in a way that also increases our productivity and engagement.

WHAT IF . . . FRIENDSHIPS DECREASE THE DRAMA AT WORK?

And lastly, our fears. All I had to do was mention that my next book was on friendships at work and I'd hear an immediate earful of all that could go wrong: But what if a manager waits too long to fire someone because of their friendship? Or hires someone because of that friendship? What if two colleagues who are friends have to compete for the same promotion? What if someone plays favoritism? What if we feel left out because two people are closer friends than we are? What if we are the boss and can't share as honestly anymore? What if I have to start supervising one of my friends? Or worse, one of them has to supervise me? What if I hire a friend and the person doesn't perform well? What if we encourage friendship but it leads to sexual harassment? What if I confide in someone and the person breaks my trust, but we still have to work together?

The irony, of course, is that those risks are already real in our workplace whether we're friends or not. We could be against friendship and have no friends, but that doesn't protect us from jealousy, gossip, drama, or feeling left out. Our boss could have no friends and it still won't stop our suspicions of favoritism or make firing someone faster and easier. Our friend could be promoted over us, but isn't that better than reporting to someone we don't admire or respect? One thing is clear: being against friendship doesn't protect our workplaces from our list of fears.

On the contrary, I'm convinced that it's in building *more* healthy relationships, not fewer, that the drama we fear will diminish.

Indeed, the lonelier we are, the less empathy we tend to feel for others, the more likely we are to take offense, the more defensive we act, and the more likely we are to hurt others by pushing them away or clinging. Avoiding the subject of friendship at work only increases the odds of unhealthy expectations, unspoken concerns, inappropriate behaviors, and lonely workers.

In the third section of this book, "How to Make Relationships Work Better for Us" (Chapters 8–12), I'll be tackling our biggest fears and teaching us new ways for showing up at work so we can increase the chances of meaningful connection while decreasing the chances of hurt feelings, angst, and rejection.

WHAT IF . . . FRIENDSHIPS AT WORK BENEFITED ALL OF US?

"I'm not here to make friends" is not only a shortsighted philosophy that has permeated a lot of work cultures, but it's also frequently heard on competitive reality TV shows followed by the words, "I'm here to win."

And it would be one thing if those people actually won and we had to talk about whether it was worth winning and being lonely. But they don't.[7] Uttering those words might sound as though we're focused on what matters most (and therefore more likely to accomplish that mission), but that motto actually increases our chances of losing the competition we claim is our priority. And it endears us to no one along the way.

It's time to let go of our hesitations, guilt, and fear about friendships at work and instead see that the more connected we are the better it is for all of us. I very much want this book to be a win-win-win for us. If we have friends at work:

- *we* will win because we'll be happier and healthier because we love our jobs and the people with whom we work;
- *our companies* (and their missions and profits) will win because we'll call in sick less, have fewer accidents, and treat their customers better because we feel connected to our teams and skilled in interpersonal relationships; and
- *our world* will win because we'll be decreasing the amount of loneliness that is plaguing us individually, and collectively.

For too long we've believed that either work will suffer from the act of socializing and the supposed "drama" that we associate with friendships, or conversely, that our friendships will feel strangled if they are tied up with work issues.

What if instead of believing that workplace friendships hurt one or the other, we were open to believing that they could actually help both? In the next chapter I am going to show you how important friendships are to you personally, especially the ones at work, and in the following chapter we'll get deeper into the research on how those friendships benefit our organizations. Both are important.

Hopefully soon, we'll be hearing a lot more of us say at work, "I'm here to make friends."

PART 1

Why Relationships Matter at Work

1

How We Benefit from Friendships at Work

Allyson confided in me that "even though nearly everyone else who works here is a millennial like I am, it's having the opposite affect I had hoped." She had gone into a job at a magazine, eight months prior, thinking that being surrounded with people in a similar life stage would help her make friends. But instead of the resonance she expected to feel, she confessed that it felt more judgmental and competitive as they all seemed to feel pressure to outdo each other. "It's almost like we each have to magnify our differences, no matter how small they are, to convince the powers-that-be that we are each the coolest and most reliable representation for our generation!" Her exhaustion in trying to stand out left her wondering who her people were, if not her age group.

Similarly, Drew expected to feel an instant camaraderie when he joined a team of engineers in Austin. While, for the most part, they had a lot in common—mostly men, engineer backgrounds, transplants to Texas, and similar temperaments—he was quick to assure me that while they were all nice, he had no idea how to connect with them. "It's pretty quiet in the offices," he said. "Everyone is polite and friendly, but they all seem eager to do their work and go home." With most of their energy and skills being devoted all day to strategic thinking, problem solving, and data analyzing, they weren't naturally prone to prioritize connection and getting to know one another. He wondered if his choice in profession doomed him to a career surrounded by people who were "in their heads all the time."

On the opposite side of the spectrum, in a workplace filled with Ping-Pong balls, music, free lunches, and hosted happy hours, Prisha wasn't having much luck either, despite what seemed like obvious commonalities with her coworkers. "We all chose to move here to the Silicon Valley, so you'd think that choice alone would basically self-select people like me—ambitious, business minded, progressive, highly educated, and committed to social change—and ensure that we could all be friends if we wanted?" She ended the sentence with the heightened sound of a question mark, basically begging me to agree with her. But my answer was unimportant because it couldn't change the fact that while she felt grateful for what seemed like a cool job, all the perks in the world weren't producing the relationships that made her feel like she belonged.

When we interview for a job, whether we do it consciously or not, we are looking around and asking, "Are there people here like me?" For as much as we might want to stand out, we also want to fit in because we assume that will lead to us feeling like we belong. In Chapter 3 I'll share what actually *does* lead to belonging—if not just being around people who are similar to us—but first let's understand why it matters so much.

Belonging is one of the, if not the most, basic human needs we share. One of the foremost authorities in the world on the study of social neuroscience, Dr. Matthew Liberman, goes so far as to say, "Maslow had it wrong." In his reference to Maslow's hierarchy of needs, which traditionally puts things like food, water, and shelter as the foundation of basic human needs, Dr. Liberman says in his book, *Social: Why Our Brains Are Wired to Connect*, that to get it right we have to move social needs to the bottom of the pyramid because an infant actually cannot get food, water, and shelter without being in a caring relationship. He says, "Love and belonging might seem like a convenience we can live without, but our biology is built to thirst for connection because it is linked to our most basic survival needs." In his study of the brain, he concludes that every other need we have is built on the bedrock of our relationships.

Unfortunately, too many of us lack that bedrock.

WHAT IS LONELINESS?

Despite the stigma, loneliness is not about being a recluse or hermit, has nothing to do with social skills, and isn't a reflection of whether someone is liked or admired. It is not the same thing as being alone, living alone, or preferring alone time. It doesn't even have to do with how many friends someone reports having. Loneliness is the perception that we are not known, supported, or loved as much as we want to be. It's wanting more belonging than we currently are experiencing.

Loneliness can occur from *lack of interaction*, but for most of us, especially those of us in the workforce, our loneliness stems more from *lack of intimacy*. In fact, most of us know plenty of people, are more networked than we've ever been, and can spend most of our time serving people or being around them—and yet we're still reporting loneliness because those interactions don't feel meaningful. It's often less about needing to know more people and more about wanting to feel known by the ones we've already met. That's why we can sometimes feel the loneliest at our company holiday party or come home peopled-out after a long day of customer service but still be dying from loneliness.

But loneliness isn't inherently bad. The feeling of loneliness is simply our body's way of telling us that we have more capacity in our lives for more connection. It's only bad if we ignore it. I love how Dr. John T. Cacioppo—one of the leading neuroscientists in the world, who studied and wrote on loneliness before his recent death and is the author of the book so aptly titled *Loneliness*—likens the experience of loneliness to hunger, thirst, or exhaustion. Just as hunger pangs inform us that we need to fuel our bodies, a dry mouth reminds us to hydrate, and yawns can motivate us to get the sleep we need, feeling lonely means our body is working well as it informs us that we function best when we feel seen and supported.[1]

Our goal then isn't to never feel lonely, just as we don't need to avoid ever feeling hungry, but rather it is to more quickly identify what that loneliness means and how we can go about getting that need met in healthy ways.

But before we can get the need met, we have to realize we have the need.

WHO'S LONELY?

So, if loneliness is the feeling of not having the relationships, or interactions, that we want, we can clearly see that all of us are prone to feel it at times. The bigger question then is how many of us are feeling this absence more regularly without being able to respond to that hunger with meaningful connection when we need it. While it's a hard feeling to admit or measure, researchers have been diligent in recent years to help quantify an experience that can feel somewhat subjective.

One of the leading voices in giving numbers to this feeling has become Cigna, who surveyed more than twenty thousand U.S. adults two years ago and concluded then (using the UCLA Loneliness scale, which is the highest standard in the industry) that, indeed, "most Americans are considered lonely."[2] Unfortunately, this year they followed up with a report revealing that our numbers have only gone up in that short time—we're now at 61 percent of us scoring as lonely, compared to 54 percent just two years ago.[3]

More specifically, that translates to almost 40 percent of us not feeling like we have close personal relationships with other people, more than 50 percent of us feeling alone or left out often, and nearly 60 percent of us not feeling like anyone knows us well. More extreme, about a quarter of us report that we rarely, or never, feel close to anyone and believe that no one understands us.

If we indeed need connections with others like we need food and water, then roughly half of us are socially malnourished, and a quarter of us are starving. Add to that number all of us who are just hungry for more nourishing relationships with the people we call friends, and the vast majority of us could do with greater social health. The human need to be seen, to be understood, to be known—by at least *someone*—isn't being met in the way we're now living our lives.

Unfortunately, that loneliness doesn't automatically disappear when we get to work. While the Cigna report shows that the majority of us are satisfied with our relationships at work and tend to be less lonely if we're in the workforce, nearly one in three of us nonetheless reports feeling disconnected from others while at work or the need to "hide our true self" at work. By another count, Imperative, a peer-coaching platform, reports that 49 percent of us feel we lack meaningful relationships at work.[4] And when I asked, "Do you ever feel lonely at work?" while only about 20 percent of us feel it frequently, nearly 60 percent of us admit to feeling it at least half the time.

	Never	*Sometimes*	*About Half the Time*	*Often*	*Always*
Overall Average	12%	27%	40%	18%	3%

This lack of social health in our workplaces isn't just in the United States either. Research out of the UK shows 60 percent of employees there suffering from loneliness at work,[5] and a recent report in Australia puts them at 40 percent.[6] Those aren't small numbers. In fact, the World Health Organization now lists "social support networks" as a determinant of health because of how many countries are seeing the impact of loneliness among their people. Unsurprisingly, certain industries and professions lend themselves to an increased chance of loneliness: entertainment (including sports, music, film, and publishing), personal care, agriculture/industry (including automotive and food and beverage), research, clinical workers, and those who are focused on out-of-office sales. Further, we're more likely to be lonely if we rely on the "gig economy," work remotely, own our own business, or are at a publicly traded company. Digging deeper in the data, it's important to note that while loneliness is affecting us all, there are certain demographics that report higher numbers:[7]

- **Men,** who tend to feel they have to hide more of who they are at work, are about 10 percent more likely than women to feel "alienated from their coworkers," "abandoned" by others when under pressure, and report feeling a "general sense of emptiness when at work."
- **New hires** and **entry-level workers** are lonelier than those with more experience or long tenure. Unsurprisingly, nearly two-thirds of those who have worked somewhere less than six months report experiencing isolation.
- **Hispanic and African American workers** are more likely (37 percent and 30 percent, respectively, versus 25 percent of whites) to feel "abandoned by coworkers when under pressure at work" and are more likely to feel alienated.
- **Those with poor or fair physical or mental health** are lonelier than those in good health. Compared to those in good health, we are about 8 points lonelier if we have fair or poor physical health, and 12 points lonelier if we have fair or poor mental health. Further, we're less likely to be lonely if we feel we're getting "just the right amount" of sleep and physical activity.

- **Senior leaders** are lonelier than their direct reports. Nearly 56 percent of leaders feel like there's no one they can talk to, and up to 69 percent feel like no one really knows them well.
- **Our youngest generations** are lonelier than our oldest. The ones who will be making up the majority of our workforce in the not-too-distant future—Generation Z (born mostly in the mid-1990s and the early 2000s) and Millennials (born mostly in the mid-1980s and 1990s)—rated themselves the loneliest. Close to 70 percent of them report feeling shy and feeling like no one really knows them well. The term FOMO—fear of missing out—is not only a Millennial cliché; it's also their experience. Loneliness is the number one fear of young people today—ranking ahead of losing a home or a job.[8] One survey showed that 42 percent of Millennial women were more afraid, by double digits compared to other generations, of loneliness than a cancer diagnosis.[9]

And while that might sound extreme to some of us, it's not without good reason.

WE'RE DYING OF LONELINESS

While loneliness isn't yet listed as a cause of death by the World Health Organization, our former US Surgeon General, Dr. Vivek Murthy, recently wrote in an aptly titled article "Work and the Loneliness Epidemic" that "during my years caring for patients, the most common pathology I saw was not heart disease or diabetes; it was loneliness."[10] With heart disease and diabetes currently ranking number one and number five, respectively, for deaths around the world, his comparison is no small statement. In fact, loneliness increases your risk of heart disease by 30 percent.[11]

Results from a huge study published in the journal *PLOS Medicine* show that lonely people are 50 percent more likely to die prematurely than those with healthy relationships. The researchers analyzed data from 148 previously published longitudinal studies that measured frequency of human interaction and tracked health outcomes for a period of seven and a half years on average, and they concluded that if we feel disconnected, unsupported, or lonely, the damage done by the lack of those relationships is:

- equivalent to smoking fifteen cigarettes a day,
- equivalent to being a lifelong alcoholic,
- more harmful than not exercising, and
- twice as harmful as obesity.[12]

Loneliness has also been associated with weaker bone density, worsened cognitive function, lower immune strength, more depression and anxiety, longer recoveries from surgery, increased risk of suicide, and the list goes on. Diseases such as cancer, stroke, and respiratory disease are correlated to the health of our relationships more than to any other factor in our lives, including such things as our diet, exercise, or even genetics.

To that point, another world-renowned physician and author, Dr. Dean Ornish, studied all the data on how significant relationships are to our health, and he concluded in his book *Love and Survival*:

> This association between social and community ties and premature death was found to be independent of and a more powerful predictor of health and longevity than age, gender, race, socioeconomic status, self-reported physical health status, and health practices such as smoking, alcoholic beverage consumption, overeating, physical activity, and utilization of preventative health services as well as a cumulative index of health practices.[13]

In fact, he noted that while someone who practices healthy lifestyle habits *and* interacts in meaningful relationships will live longer, on average, than someone who does only one or the other, what might surprise a few of us is that those with *unhealthy* lifestyles but strong social ties were two to three times less likely to die, during their follow-up almost twenty years later, than those who ate healthy and exercised but felt lonely.[14]

We have for too long put an emphasis on treadmills over telephone calls and kale smoothies over connecting. Our health magazines and most fitness gurus haven't quite caught up to this truth—they still seem to focus on toned muscles and losing weight—but the research is becoming more and more irrefutable that our relationships, or lack of them, are playing a starring role in our health. We're going to dive deeper into understanding what about our relationships impacts our health in a moment, but let's first make sure that we know what we're talking about when we use the word *lonely*.

FRIENDSHIPS AT WORK FOR OUR HEALTH

Why does our loneliness impact our health so much? The short answer is that healthy relationships put our bodies in a more relaxed mode; as we feel supported and loved, our bodies move out of stress and into repair and recovery.

But I want to share with you the long answer, too, because these reports and studies better reinforce this truth in our minds when we can understand *exactly* how our relationships function in this healing way.

Relationships Decrease Worry and Increase Resiliency

The first example of how relationships bolster our health is the well-known psychology study that reveals how we assess life differently when a friend is nearby. Students, some standing alone and others standing with a friend next to them, all wear a heavy backpack at the bottom of a hill and are asked to estimate the steepness of the incline. The results are reliable: those standing alone conclude the hill to be steeper than those standing with friends.[15]

Perhaps the outcome sounds simple and obvious, but let the truth of that one sink in for a moment. How many of us feel exhausted or weary by life or work? How many of us feel overwhelmed? How many of us feel like the metaphorical hill in front of us looks too steep? If there was a way to face life so our perception was radically changed to see our situations as easier, less intimidating, and more doable, wouldn't you want it? Interestingly, the research also showed that the more intimate and meaningful the friendship, the less steep the hill was perceived; and that conversely, when subjects were asked to think of a neutral or disliked person, they estimated the hill to be even steeper.

Similarly, taking it to the workplace, a study published by O.C. Tanner found that 75 percent of us who have a best friend at work say we feel we're able to "take anything on" compared to only 58 percent of those who don't have a best friend at work.[16] That relationship translates to almost a 20 percentage point increase in our belief that we can take on big challenges!

Relationships Protect Our Bodies from Stress

The next study I want to share is similar but shows us what that "less steep hill" actually looks like in our brain. In this one, subjects were placed in an MRI machine where they received intermittent mild electrical shocks. Not knowing when the shocks were going to occur, this test showed the brain's response to our anticipatory anxiety, the type of stress so many of us live with as we worry about all the things that are uncertain. As cortisol, the stress chemical, shot into the brain, several splotches of red lit up the MRI brain image scan where stress was being processed. But contrast that with those subjects who were invited to hold the hand of someone they loved sitting outside the MRI machine. This time, instead of red splotches popping up all over the scan, only three small dots of brain activity lit up—which was less than a third of what was triggered when they were alone.[17]

In this case, like that of the hill, the stressors don't change: the hill is still as steep, and they are still being mildly shocked with electricity, whether they have a friend nearby or not. The only thing that changes is their experience of that stress. In one case, their friendship prompts them to feel less worried and more hopeful; in the other, their relationship serves as a protective barrier to feeling the stress of life. Dr. James Coan, the lead researcher in this study and a neuroscientist at the University of Virginia, talked in an interview about the burden of coping with life's stressors: "When you have to deal with them all by yourself, it not only feels more exhausting, it literally creates more wear on your body."[18]

"It literally creates more wear on your body." In other words, feeling supported acts as a buffer that protects our bodies from the impact and damage that we know results from stress. Interestingly, even holding the hand of a stranger helped the participants feel calmer, though the deeper the relationship, the less unpleasant the shocks were perceived.

Do you have stress in your work? Mild shocks that are silently and slowly draining energy in your life? Would you feel hopeful knowing there was a way to protect your body from that breakdown? Wish you had a hand to hold that could alleviate some of the anxiety and mental pressure?

Having friendships in our lives doesn't eliminate our stress, but it does prevent us from absorbing the destruction that often comes with it.

Relationships Reduce Disease and Strengthen Immune Function

My first illustration of the steep hill was about how relationships hinder or help us perceive stress in our lives, and my second was about how those relationships change the chemicals in our brain. The last point I want to provide on the health front is to look inside our bodies through the microscope and showcase just how impactful our loneliness is, even when it comes to germs and infectious disease, cancer, or coronary heart disease. Because most of our practice of medicine in the last couple hundred years has functioned from our understanding of germs, it's hard for us to fathom how our relationships might make a difference to diseases that seem to require surgeries, pharmaceuticals, and even chemotherapy.

But because of the amazing work of researchers and social epidemiologists, we're starting to see just how significant our societal factors are in determining not only whether we'll recover from certain diseases but whether they can be prevented in the first place! For example, something like cholesterol, which we so often think is simply a diet and exercise issue, is affected by our relationships in that how our body metabolizes our cholesterol is shaped, in part, by how much stress our body is under and how supported we feel.[19] In fact, in one study of 2,300 men who had survived a heart attack, those who had low stress and high connection were less than four times likely to die than those who were high stress and low connection. Social isolation adds stress on our bodies and makes them more fertile for disease.[20]

One study of women with metastatic breast cancer tracked all the varietal factors (including smoking, diet, exercise, marriage) to determine the difference between those who survived the diagnosis versus those who didn't. You know where this is going . . . the only factor that doubled their life expectancy was having a consistent circle of support.[21]

Even something like defending against the common cold comes down to our relationships—and in this case the diversity of our relationships. In one study in which everyone was infected with the virus, it mattered more how many of the twelve different types of relationships people had (that is, work, family, neighbors, schoolmates) than the overall number of relationships. Those with only one to three types of relationships were four times more likely of developing the cold than those who reported six or more types of relationships. Diversity in our relationships makes a difference—our work friends contribute to our health.[22]

Our relationships build up our immune system and strengthen our body's ability to fight diseases that we once thought were simply cut-and-dry, cause-and-effect issues. The medical community is now seeing loneliness as a predictor for diseases—diabetes, coronary heart disease, and influenza, to name a few—and as a determining factor for our chances of recovery.

In short, whether our stress shows up as a steep hill that looks hopeless and overwhelming, as intermittent electrical shocks that cause worry and anxiety, or as our bodies being fertile soil ripe for diseases such as coronary heart disease or breast cancer is determined, first and foremost, in how we answer the question "How loved and supported do I feel?"

And while I hope you can look at your neighbors, friends, and family and say a convincing "very supported," the truth is that we're 78 percent more likely to spend more time with our colleagues than our nonwork friends,[23] so if we can't say that about where we work, then chances are high that our health is taking a huge hit.

RELATIONSHIPS BOOST HAPPINESS

But we don't only want to be healthy, we also want to be happy.

Think for a moment about all the things you want to achieve, experience, or own (for example, cars, promotions, big bank accounts, specific body weights, more square footage) and then remember this: that entire list adds up to less than a third of your overall happiness.

The truth is that if you want to make a substantial difference to your happiness, invest your energy and resources where it truly matters most: your relationships. David Niven was in the basement of the library at Ohio State University looking across mountains of research reports that would never reach the people who most needed them when he decided to start compiling and translating all the research into practical advice. In his book *The 100 Simple Secrets of Happy People: What Scientists Have Learned and How You Can Use It*, he summarizes, "Contrary to the belief that happiness is hard to explain, or that it depends on having great wealth, researchers have identified the core factors in a happy life. The primary components are number of friends, closeness of friends, closeness of family, and relationships with co-workers and neighbors. Together these features explain about 70 percent of personal happiness."[24]

Seventy percent of our happiness comes down to our relationships—including our coworkers. In fact, see what a specific difference we admit a best friend at work can make:

Are you happy at work?					
	Almost Never	*Occasionally*	*About Half the Time*	*Often*	*Almost Always*
Have Best Friend	3%	6%	12%	31%	48%
No Best Friend	2%	19%	27%	30%	22%

Look at that last column—that's more than a 100 percent increase in happiness for having a best friend at work. If we have a best friend at work, we report an 80 percent chance of being happy often or almost always.

But we've known this for a long time. In a landmark book, American political scientist Robert D. Putnam published *Bowling Alone* in 2000, which highlighted the decline of our social culture. He said even back then, "Many studies have shown that social connections with coworkers are a strong predictor—some would say the strongest single predictor—of job satisfaction." And he concluded, "People with friends at work are happier at work."[25]

FRIENDSHIP FOR OUR WORK SATISFACTION

Happier at work, indeed. If we're lonely, two-thirds of us feel it's negatively impacting our mental health and over a third of us feel it affects our ability to do our jobs.[26] How we feel about the people we work with is directly correlated to how much we enjoy our job and life.

In the book *Wellbeing: The 5 Essential Elements,* Tom Rath and Jim Harter share the results of a study of people in more than 150 countries and conclude that the "single best predictor" for well-being is enjoying how we spend our days, and more to the point is it depends on "not *what* people are doing—but *who* they are with."[27]

Read that line again. More important than *what* we are doing all day long is *who* is with us in the doing of it. Our self-reporting for what brings us joy matches completely with what the medical community is saying matters most, too: our relationships.

The most stressful and high-responsibility job can be rewarding *if* one feels supported, part of a team, engaged, believed in, cheered for, and appreciated. And the least stressful and low-responsibility jobs can slowly seep our energy if we don't get enough social interaction or have to navigate mostly negative interactions. No job description can be perfect enough to make up for a critical or negligent boss, exhausting coworkers, a chilly social atmosphere, complaining customers, or nonexpressed appreciation. We know this to be true in our own lives: we will be miserable at our "dream job" if we can't stand who we work with, and conversely, we'll stay in a role we don't like all that much if we love our coworkers and boss.

As I've been working with teams to help them improve their relationships with each other, I've continued to find on the *Healthy Team Relationship Assessment* that those who have friends score the health of their team higher than their teammates who have no friends. They have the same leader and same coworkers, yet their experience of their team differs by more than twelve points.

Number of Friends on Team	*Average Overall Satisfaction on Team*
0	65.8
1	68.5
2	77.1
3+	78.2

You want to enjoy your work more, in general, and your team more, specifically? Make a few friends.

Relationships Lead to Job Engagement

And it's not just friends, in general, but "best friends" that matter most. We are up to seven times more likely to feel engaged in our work if we have at least one "best friend at work," reports Gallup. In contrast, without a best friend, we only have a 1 in 12 chance of feeling engaged.[28] Certainly, our companies care about our engagement, as it is directly linked to our performance, but from our vantage point, it also translates to fewer sick days, more confidence to express our ideas and suggestions, and more positive energy in the office.

Now here, when the word *best* shows up, is where most of us have the biggest objections.

And while this book isn't specifically about making *best friends* at work (though the last chapter is devoted to that), this is as good a time as any to remind us all that *best* isn't about a *quantity* that only one friend in our entire lives can be called; it's about a *quality* of relationship that we can build with several. We can, and should, have a handful of healthy, good as it gets, friends. And, ideally, at least one at work.

Look how much our chances go down of feeling lonely at work if we have that best friend:

	Never Lonely	*Sometimes Lonely*	*About Half the Time*	*Often Lonely*	*Always Lonely*
Have Best Friend	25%	33%	35%	6%	0%
No Best Friend	5%	20%	38%	30%	7%

Obviously, loneliness is more than just one best friend, but without a best friend, we have a 37 percent chance of being often or always lonely; whereas just one friend drops that number to 6 percent.

Jackson, a twenty-something, who answered my *Friendship in the Workplace Survey*, summed it up when he said, "Having a best friend at work is not only more fun [because I] have someone to goof off with a bit and share stories with, but he basically leaves me feeling like someone has my back." He followed that up with examples of what helped him feel supported: "If I miss a meeting, feel discouraged, or can't think of a solution to a problem . . . I know I can rely on him." Certainly, in an ideal world, our managers and coworkers could offer that same feeling, but unfortunately, too many of us feel like our bosses are the ones we most need protecting from, and nearly every person I know has a story of a coworker that does anything but support.

To that point, Rochelle, who works in the public library system, says, "At my current workplace, cross-team collaboration and communication are awful. It's every department for themselves, and it feels like we're all in competition with each other, vying for praise from our director. I don't feel respected by my colleagues because they're all so busy trying to throw me (and others) under the bus to make themselves look good. I'm exhausted." She's quick to point out that while this would be disheartening for her in any environment, she has been shocked that it's this blatant at a nonprofit, whose mission isn't even to make money but simply to serve.

Feeling connected, or not, to those with whom we work regularly shows up as the number one factor for our job satisfaction, as you'll see in the next chapter. But so far, the data is clear: if you want to like your job, feel better physically, increase your mental and emotional health, and report greater happiness and energy, then make a close friend at work.

2

How Our Company Benefits from Our Friendships at Work

Unfortunately, very few managers, HR professionals, or corporate legal teams are lying awake at night trying to figure out how to bond more people in their organizations. I can attest that they aren't Googling "friendship speaker" or "how to encourage friendships at work." But they should be.

We all should be because the challenges we are stressed about—such as increasing employee engagement, building a diverse workforce that gets along, maximizing the productivity of our employees, lowering stress and burnout, recruiting talented employees who fit our culture, training for better customer service, decreasing healthcare costs, encouraging collaboration and creativity, addressing employee drug use, preparing for workplace violence, preventing sexual harassment, developing stronger leaders, and reducing employee turnover—all have healthy relationships at their core.

Every single one of those objectives comes down to the personal and relational health of the people we employ.

And even more pointedly, to how they like, enjoy, and respect those with whom they work. A new report, "Well-Being in the Workplace," recently released from the Myers-Briggs Company, showcases the findings from a three-year international study of more than ten thousand people in 131 countries and confirms that "relationships are the leading contributor to workplace well-being."[1]

The leading contributor. I wasn't shocked at all that our relationships were one of the biggest contributors to our satisfaction at work—Gallup started tracking that outcome a generation ago—but to see, again, that relationships edged out other crucial factors, such as job meaning, personal accomplishments, engagement, and positive emotions, is still hard to really believe.

It's their relationships *at* work that matter most while they're there. While employee satisfaction is not one factor alone, it is nearly impossible to attain it if our employees feel alone. Their relationships *to each other* continue to score higher than we're collectively admitting. So even if we could assume that every employee walking in our front doors each day was getting their relational needs met outside of work (which they aren't), it wouldn't be enough. Unfortunately, too many of them are arriving at work lonely, feeling lonely while they're in our care, and going back home even more lonely and stressed.

We have the incredible opportunity to disrupt that cycle in a way that serves our missions and boosts our bottom line.

THE COST OF LONELINESS ON PROFITABILITY

It can be a tricky game to try to put a precise price tag on loneliness in our workforce, particularly as there's a range of how lonely we all are, a host of problems when trying to measure it, and a variety of ways it gets expressed on the job. But ask those who are lonely and more than a third of them blatantly admit that it results in them making more mistakes, feeling less productive, and getting sick more often.[2]

That adds up. In fact, as the UK was the first country to appoint a Minister of Loneliness, in 2018, they've been pioneering some great research on the topic in general but also more specifically on how loneliness affects our business costs. They've looked at such things as how loneliness affects employee health outcomes, the costs associated with absence due to sickness, how it affects employee well-being, and the price tag to employers in loss of productivity and voluntary staff turnover. They've conservatively estimated that their lonely workers are costing employers upwards of £2.5 billion ($3.5 billion) and conclude, "Our findings of substantial costs from loneliness to UK employers strongly suggest that it is in their interests to take both reactive and preventative approaches to minimise [sic] the loneliness of their employees."[3]

Let's break that down a bit and dive a bit deeper in some of the metrics that are correlated with our loneliness at work, starting with one of the biggest headaches for leaders and HR professionals: employee retention and turnover.

Employee Engagement and Retention

Sherri, a COO at a hospital, felt sick realizing that turnover was costing them almost $10 million a year, so knowing that their savings could be significant if they could increase their retention by even a few percentage points she went to her HR team and asked, "What can we do?"

One of their big ideas was to put together a campaign to encourage more friendships at work. Sherri later told me, "I rolled my eyes and thought 'they've got to be kidding me,' but then they showed me the research and we ended up reaching our retention goals last year."

Of course, when giving notice, no one says, "I'm leaving because I'm lonely," but Workhuman reports that the more friends we have at work, the less likely we are to take another job offer, whereas even one friend doubles the likelihood of employees saying they "love" their company and are proud to work there. (Interestingly, that number continues to increase as their number of reported friends increases.) And these aren't employees who just stay longer, but they are also more trusting of leadership and report feeling significantly more engaged.[4]

What does that engagement look like? According to Gallup, the company that has long been tracking the connection between friendship and engagement, "An organization full of employees who believe they belong is an organization full of employees who feel purposeful, inspired and alive—in other words, engaged."[5] Employees with a best friend at work are:

- 43 percent more likely to report having received praise or recognition for their work in the last seven days.
- 37 percent more likely to report that someone at work encourages their development.
- 35 percent more likely to report coworker commitment to quality.
- 28 percent more likely to report that, in the last six months, someone at work has talked to them about their progress.
- 27 percent more likely to report that the mission of their company makes them feel their job is important.
- 27 percent more likely to report that their opinions seem to count at work.
- 21 percent more likely to report that, at work, they have the opportunity to do what they do best every day.[6]

All these numbers drive engagement and retention, which adds up to more profitability. We increase the number of workers who feel connected to a best friend and we increase the likelihood of them feeling connected to their job.

Our employees need to hear a strong *yes* when they ask, "Do I belong *here*?"

Employee Compensation

Even throwing money at them doesn't make as big of a difference as fostering their friendships.

A study across Europe found that even though half of employees feel underpaid, the majority of them said they'd turn down a pay raise if it meant working with someone they didn't like. When asked why they stay at their current job, their number one answer—even before things such as enjoying their role, the development of their career, or being good at their job—was, "I have a good relationship with my colleagues."[7] Similarly, Workhuman reports that US professionals rank compensation as the third most important factor, following behind enjoying the people we work with when answering why we stay at our companies.[8] And numerous studies are showing that this value for belonging at work scores even higher for Generation Z and Millennials.

We can't underpay our employees, but we have to remember that giving a raise not only doesn't solve the issue of their disengagement, but it costs us even more if that employee stays disengaged. LinkedIn Learning has put together an employee disengagement calculator built on the data that 17.2 percent of an organization's workforce is disengaged and that disengaged employees cost their organization 34 percent of their salary. That means if you have five thousand employees with a median salary of $60,000, the total cost of disengagement to your organization comes out to $17.5 million a year.[9] Not a cheap price tag, at all. So while a disengaged employee earning $60,000 a year will cost $20,400, a salary increase to $80,000 now costs $27,200 a year if the person is still disengaged.

Let's compensate them *and* connect them.

Employee Health, Safety, and Resilience

The health of our employees, if they are lonely, is at greater risk than if they are chain-smokers, obese, or addicted to alcohol. But what we care about more than our average employee might care about is how that translates to five fewer sick days a year and almost half as many workplace accidents.[10] Employees with friends have stronger immune systems, lower rates of anxiety and depression, recover from surgeries faster, and show up to work with more energy.

Motivated by the desire to create a safer workplace, one CEO of a construction company brought me in to teach relationships to his employees—mostly men, a mix of engineers, architects, and cement pourers. He guessed that most of those men, on their own, weren't going to go sign up for a "friendship class." But by teaching them relationship skills in his work setting, he not only built a stronger and safer workforce who could use those skills to his direct benefit; but it was to his indirect benefit when they fostered better relationships at home too. "Honestly," he said, "the happier they are at home means they show up at work happier too." Six months later, he chuckled as he shared with me that he still overhears guys saying to each other, "Remember, Shasta said we need to practice sharing our lives with each other." They wanted that connection; they just needed permission and training.

Men, who on average die younger than women, also happen to usually report feeling lonelier than women and having fewer best friends. I'm guessing there's a correlation. What we teach all of our employees at work can improve the health of their lives in every way. If we facilitate the connections that humans need during the day (or whenever our employees work), then we can go to sleep at night knowing we're lengthening the lives, boosting the health, reducing the stress, and strengthening the mental health of humanity in general, instead of being the ones blamed for their burnout, exhaustion, and poor health.

For Sherri, the hospital COO, she knew that to lower turnover and increase engagement meant increasing the resilience of those in her care. "Our associates are exposed to pain, death, and trauma every day," she said. "We realized it's not just keeping people in our system but helping them recover from the stress of their jobs fast enough to be able to stay here." And as we saw in the last chapter, it's through relationships that we protect our bodies from absorbing the stress, feel more hopeful, and strengthen our mental health.

Employee Innovation and Collaboration

But we don't just want our people healthy and staying forever if we don't feel like they are also showing up with creativity, innovation, and the ability to collaborate. Enter Google's famous "Project Aristotle" study in which they spent years studying teams with the hopes of discovering what made the difference between high- and low-performing teams. It's one thing to simply assign a bunch of people to a project or task and quite another to have the confidence that they'll maximize their collective strengths, consider diverse ideas, and take the risks to pursue big ideas.

We'll unpack their results a bit more in the next chapter, but suffice it to say here: we now know that the secret to teams is what Harvard Business School professor Amy Edmondson calls "psychological safety," which she defines as "a shared belief held by members of a team that the team is safe for interpersonal risk taking."[11]

Interpersonal risk taking doesn't happen in a vacuum without trust. And it doesn't happen with people we fear will judge us or our differing ideas. Psychological safety rests on a foundation of healthy relationships—people who know how to communicate well, empathize with each other, and who feel that they can rely on one another. It's one thing to recruit and hire talent, but if our people don't know how to bump into each other and allow themselves to be impacted by those around them to create something bigger than one of them—then we're leaving big ideas and money on the table.

In fact, look at the seven statements used to help measure whether a team has psychological safety and see if you think there's one that doesn't come down to healthy relationships.

- If you make a mistake on this team, it is often held against you.
- Members of this team are able to bring up problems and tough issues.
- People on this team sometimes reject others for being different.
- It is safe to take a risk on this team.
- It is difficult to ask other members of this team for help.
- No one on this team would deliberately act in a way that undermines my efforts.

- Working with members of this team, my unique skills and talents are valued and utilized.[12]

A team, of course, is nothing if not the strength of the relationship between its members. They don't have to be best friends, but as you'll see in the next chapter, you certainly want them to exhibit the outcome of a healthy friendship in which everyone has the skills to connect in helpful ways. Which leads us to our next point.

Employee Interpersonal Skills and Customer Service

Without a doubt, the biggest growth (an 83 percent jump from 49 million to 90 million![13]) in our job market since 1980 is in jobs requiring stronger social skills. And by social skills we mean interpersonal, communication, and management skills. Gone are the days when we can simply put our head down and grunt our way through our work. Fewer of us can show up and get our job done merely by being present or flexing our muscles. To that point, Minouche Shafik, the director of the London School of Economics, articulated in 2018 that "in the past, jobs were about muscles, now they're about brains, but in the future they'll be about the heart."[14] I'd argue we're in that future already. In a report by Pew Research titled "The State of American Jobs," when workers are asked about which skills we rely on most in our jobs, the top of the list was interpersonal skills, critical thinking, and good written and spoken communications skills.[15]

And what I found most interesting is that while more and more of us might describe our jobs as "sitting behind a computer," only a third of us say computer skills are central to the work we do. And since most of us tend to just repeat the same technical skills in the same small handful of software applications, the stress of learning technical skills is far more intermittent than the ongoing issues we have with the people we work beside.

These interpersonal skills we say matter most to our job success need to be taught in our workplaces. If we want our workforce treating our customers better, understanding how to sell more effectively, participating in collaborative efforts, or speaking up for what they need and what ideas they have—it's going to fall on our organizations to teach these skills.

I wish it weren't so. I wish I could tell you that your new employees have been well versed in interpersonal skills from their educational experiences. Unfortunately, only 8 percent of us feel we've learned these skills through our formal education. That's leaving most of us just bumping along, honing whatever skills we acquire by watching and practicing. And we all know the modeling most of us have isn't necessarily what we want replicated.

The more we focus on training relationship skills within our walls, the more we are equipping our workforce with the skills that broaden our walls. The same three skills that foster healthy friendships with our colleagues and managers are the same skills that strengthen the relationships the company depends upon with its clients, vendors, stockholders, and potential customers.

The bottom line of every company—from leadership training to team building, from research and development to sales and marketing—rests upon our ability to know how to build, deepen, and repair relationships.

- Too many companies use their social media platforms more as one-directional megaphones rather than as a tool for building relationships with their current and potential customers.
- Too many employees describe their off-site meetings as either boring or simply fun diversions, rather than as a strategic experience designed to deepen the team engagement.
- Too many board members and leaders interact as though schmoozing is what bonds people, rather than learning what actually creates a healthy bond and practicing those authentic behaviors.

- Too many customer service representatives see their job as simply trying to put out the fire as fast as they can, rather than stepping into the opportunity to deepen a relationship with a customer.
- Too many supervisors treat their vendors as hired hands, rather than with the intention to deepen the loyalty and build more trust.
- Too many designers and advertisers run toward "How do we show off this product?" rather than asking the more significant question, "What would build our relationship best with our target audience?"

The truth is that once we teach our employees how to build healthy relationships, then we have given them the key to know how to deepen all the relationships our companies depend upon for our success. If we can provide intentional opportunities to help them practice those skills on their teams and in their departments, then we can rest assured that their social muscles are getting a workout, becoming stronger for every other relationship they experience.

THE CALL TO ORGANIZATIONS TO FOCUS ON CONNECTION

Far too few people can even articulate what a healthy relationship looks like, let alone identify exactly what actions lead to trust and bonding, and then have the positive experience of putting those into action. That's what we're going to look at in the next chapter. But before we go there, I want to call us back to our collective mission.

When we see reports stating that anywhere between 20 percent and 60 percent of our population is showing up at work with loneliness—whether from social isolation, lack of intimacy, loss of meaningful relationships in their family, an experience in their lives they feel no one understands, or from not feeling appreciated in their workplace—it is past time to teach them how to feed that hunger. If we don't, we basically have employees with serious unmet needs (similar to not getting enough sleep or not having enough food to eat) showing up with less energy, empathy, joy, and clarity.

We may not feel like this is our responsibility, but the people relying on us think otherwise.

In the *Friendships in the Workplace Survey,* 60 percent of those surveyed don't believe their employer does enough to foster their friendships at work. (Similar numbers can be found in other studies.[16]) Which would be unfortunate by itself, but it's made worse in that one in four people said their friendships, or lack of them, was "entirely" dependent upon the workplace culture around them. Add those who think the company is "probably" responsible, and that's 56 percent of our workforce who feels their friendships rely on the tone we set.

Whether I have a best friend at work is entirely dependent on the workplace culture.				
Definitely True	Probably True	I Don't Know	Probably False	Definitely False
24%	32%	16%	18%	10%

Only 10 percent don't hold us completely responsible.

And while it's good business to care for those who determine the quality of our products and services, it's also good humanity to see the opportunity we have to make a massive contribution to cure what is nothing less than a deadly epidemic.

For *where* else are we going to turn this *Titanic* around? We're not joining bowling leagues, attending church, hanging out with our neighbors, or participating in civic organizations as we used to. Work is the primary place where we are gathering. Our jobs are definitely a paycheck we need, but they are also the place where we come together to connect and make a difference. Our companies are central to our lives—they are the primary place where we meet people, the place where we spend the most time, and the place where we have the potential to be most seen for what we can offer to others.

So if our workplaces are where we can make the biggest difference to our collective health, then guess who we need helping connect us?

Yes, you.

We need you influencing your team, your department, your organization, your industry to consider how we might do business differently, better. We need you trusting the science and telling them it's okay to make friends at work. We need you trusting your heart that they need friends at work.

We need connectors who can stand in the spaces that are too quiet, too chaotic, too competitive, too toxic, too exhausting, too image conscious and help give us permission to connect in more meaningful ways.

We need supervisors who micromanage less and friendship facilitate more.

We need more human resources professionals who, instead of getting scared by all the risks of connection, get excited by the rewards that come with it too. For they will know that nothing mighty is made without risk, but they will inquire, "How can we build a stronger community to better withstand some of the risks?"

We need more visionaries in the C suites who don't just look at the people around them as resources to an end but rather as relationships for which they are responsible. For responsible you are. Whether you want to be, or not, you are the leaders of our communities today. It is around your leadership that we gather, around your workplace that we call our second home, and around your other hires that will affect our health more than any other factor. Please see how much we need you to lead us not only toward revenue, but toward relationships.

And we need you because you need us too. We know your titles can feel alienating, that your roles can leave you feeling unseen and misunderstood, and that your responsibilities have often been prioritized over the relationships you've needed too. You're not meant to lead us and then feel alone.

Connection, I promise, is good for your people, good for your business, and good for you.

PART 2

What Makes All Relationships Actually Work?

3

What Is a Friendship?

The Three Relationship Requirements

Ask most people "What is a friendship?" and you'll get answers like:

- "Someone I like."
- "Someone who makes me laugh."
- "Someone who's always there for me."
- "Someone who knows the worst of me and still loves me."
- "Someone whose shoulder I can cry on."
- "Someone I trust."
- "Someone to have fun with."

Those all sound great, but none of them are a definition by which we can measure whether we have a friendship. There are a lot of people we like, who make us laugh, and who we might even trust but with whom we never become friends. And sometimes our friends do judge us and aren't always "there" for us when we need them. So, no, those might be qualities or experiences that we appreciate in some of our friendships, but they are not requirements of all friendships, nor complete definitions.

Further, ask someone the best way to make friends and without a doubt the answer almost always comes down to "find people who you have things in common with."

Again, it sounds great, but it doesn't exactly work that way.

This is the chapter in which we define friendship and better understand exactly what forms that bond.

COMMONALITY ISN'T THE PATH TO BELONGING

It's no secret that when we interview for a job we look for people "like us," but we do the same when we are the ones hiring. Or selling. Or marketing. Or advertising. Or leading. Pretty much every action we take at work, if done with instinct, is done with some bias toward similarity.

So while I'll assume that all of us already know how important it is to get along with, talk to, and work with people who are different from us, let's still acknowledge that we are well-oiled machines at believing commonality to be synonymous with bonding, trusting, and liking others. I've seen this for years in my work: mothers believe they'll bond better with other mothers, singles assume their best friends will be other singles, and no matter our age, we tend to seek out others near our own. And while there is nothing wrong with wanting some of our friends to resonate with our current experience or identity—and as we'll soon see when we look at the Three Relationship Requirements, commonalities can sometimes play a role—it is crucial to remember that our brain is merely making up what it thinks it needs for us to feel like we belong. Our preferences say more about how we identify ourselves than they do about with whom we can form a strong and healthy friendship.

Let me repeat myself: what we think we need to have in common with someone only shows us what we want reinforced in our identity and says nothing about the potential of love, trust, and belonging between any two people.

One of my favorite studies, of the many out there in which we expect commonalities to show up as the primary bonding force, features a sociology professor who followed up with graduates from a police academy in Maryland; the study's stated goal was to identify the factors that predicted with whom the graduates would feel closest to.[1] Upon looking at the data of which cadets became friends, one might expect that bonds would have developed among those who shared ethnic background, marital status, religious affiliation, or even shared interests. We frequently assume that we're more likely to bond with someone if we both vote the same, are both parents of young kids, or both love to play hockey; but the professor's results showed that those commonalities had hardly any impact on whether any two cadets ended up becoming friends. We'll talk more about the results of this study in Chapter 6 on Consistency.

Suffice it to say that even though we tend to hire, act warmer toward, and be attracted to people whom we perceive are similar to us, repeated studies show that what we think we need to have in common with someone to trust them or like them doesn't end up bearing any weight. No weight at all, in fact. For every case of "birds of a feather flock together" is a case of "opposites attract," and the truth is that while we can now name things we have in common with our closest friends, we could also come up with just as long of a list of things we don't have in common with them. But our brains tend to focus on that which we do, which is fine for fostering that relationship, except we're then at risk of convincing ourselves we know which commonalities matter most. And we simply don't.

A study out of the University of Texas showcased our bias for assuming that people who agree with us on a variety of topics are more knowledgeable, moral, and overall better people; it also revealed the limitations of commonalities. Yes, we are prone to like people with whom we think we share commonalities, but "sharing a strong dislike of fast food, for example, was just as powerful a predictor of attraction as favoring the same political party," reported Ori Brafman and Rom Brafman in their book *Click: The Forces Behind How We Fully Engage with People, Work, and Everything We Do*. Read that quote again and let it sink in. If I had a dollar for every time someone tried to convince me that a "shared worldview" was the most important part of a healthy relationship I'd be rich, but the data doesn't back it up.

Regarding a study now frequently referred to as "The 36 Questions to Fall in Love," which provides a method for creating closeness between people, it's interesting not only that they could produce closeness between complete strangers but also that there were "no significant closeness effects" when pairs were matched for "nondisagreement on important attitudes."[2] Random strangers bonded just as much as those who were matched on what we think is important. Again, it came down to *how* they bonded more than *who* they bonded with. (We'll talk more about this study in Chapter 7 on Vulnerability.)

One last illustration of the fact that we don't need commonalities to like each other, bond, or work well together comes from the previously mentioned Project Aristotle, in which Google searched for the factors making up "the perfect team."

They initially had a really hard time identifying what made the difference between a high-performing team and one that just limped along. For every example of why one team performed well, there was another high-performing team that behaved in a completely opposite way. Combing through the data from 180 teams revealed no strong patterns of similarity. The only thing that was initially obvious was "that the 'who' part of the equation didn't seem to matter," reported Abeer Dubey, a manager in Google's People Analytics division.[3] In other words, they couldn't find predictors of success based on personalities, preferences, skills, backgrounds, schedules, or any other shared commonalities.

Our proclivity toward bias so very much wants to believe that our bonding and success comes down to who the other person is (and conversely, how much they are like us), but time and again, as hard as it is for us to believe it, the success of a relationship has less to do with finding the "right person" whom we like, and has more to do with fostering the "right relationship." In other words, healthy relationships are not so much about the *who* as the *how*.

THE PATH TO BELONGING: THE THREE REQUIREMENTS OF ALL HEALTHY RELATIONSHIPS

Then what makes a friendship if not commonalities?

In comparing the various factors that social scientists are studying when they look at how we create bonds, whom we confide in, whom we call a best friend, what makes a healthy marriage, what builds trust, or what makes up the perfect team, three factors always emerge. Any definition we develop needs to be built on the back of these three nonnegotiables. An entire chapter will be devoted to each of these specifically in the workplace, but let's start here by briefly identifying the three factors that make up every relationship.

1. **Positivity basically means positive feelings.** Positivity is the result we feel in healthy relationships as we are left feeling good from such things as pride, awe, empathy, kindness, acts of service, gratitude, laughter, and affirmation. Friendship is absolutely about two people raising the emotional happiness of each other.
2. **Consistency basically means consistent interaction.** Consistency is when we log the hours and devote the time to each other; it's how we build a shared history and make memories; it's the repetition or regularity that develops patterns, rituals, and expectations in our relationship. It's

from this consistent time that we come to predict consistent behaviors that lead to us feeling like we can rely on each other.

3. **Vulnerability basically means meaningful sharing.** Vulnerability is the sharing and revealing of who we are; it's two people choosing to get to know each other; it's allowing someone else to hear our ideas, know our opinions, validate our feelings, and listen to our experiences. Vulnerability is what leads to us ultimately feeling seen and known by another, which is required for feeling loved or respected.

Like a formula, a healthy relationship must have all three: Positivity, Consistency, and Vulnerability.

Friendship = Positivity + Consistency + Vulnerability

Everything we name and want in our relationships falls under these three categories, are descriptions of or preferences of ways we do these three actions, or are produced by these three nonnegotiables.

For example, if we say we want someone who doesn't judge us, that is the outcome that happens when we receive validation, affirmation, or empathy (Positivity actions) from someone after we share something that felt risky (Vulnerability action).

Or if we say trust is the foundation of every relationship, what we're saying is that we feel safe with that person, a feeling that is produced primarily from Consistency, because as we develop a history of interaction, we're able to rely on, or predict, how someone is going to respond, which leaves us feeling like we trust them.

Right up there, next to trust, on the list of things we say we want in friends is usually honesty. Which is really just another way of saying, you guessed it: Vulnerability.

Or if we say we want friends who know how to have fun (whether we define that by friends who surf, play video games, or like to dance), then really we're not saying anything about who we can bond with as much as we're saying how we prefer to consistently spend our time bonding. That "fun" is our way of saying we want to feel good (Positivity) as we spend time (Consistency) with others.

At the end of the day, while we might use different words, the truth remains: if we practice these three things, we *will* produce a healthy relationship. Time and time again, our social research continues to reiterate how foundational these three concepts are in our relationships. Let's look at a few.

While he uses different words, note how William Rawlins, the Stocker professor of Interpersonal Communication at Ohio University, landed on similar findings:

> I've listened to someone as young as 14 and someone as old as 100 talk about their close friends, and [there are] three expectations of a close friend that I hear people describing and valuing across the entire life course: Somebody to talk to, someone to depend on, and someone to enjoy.[4]

Did you catch the three? Someone to talk to (Vulnerability), someone to depend on (Consistency), and someone to enjoy (Positivity).

Similarly, psychologists Debra Oswald and Eddie Clark, studying "friendship maintenance behaviors," reported in the *Journal of Social and Clinical Psychology* that they found four behaviors that made a difference: openness or self-disclosure (Vulnerability), Positivity (same name), interaction and time spent together (Consistency), and supportiveness (which for my work is the result of Positivity and Consistency).[5]

Take even the conclusion of what Google's search for the perfect team revealed. After two years of rigorous study, they found what makes the difference between a good team and a dysfunctional one had:

- nothing to do with *who* was on the team (that is, how smart they were, what they had in common, their personalities), and

> nothing to do with *what* specifically that team did (that is, what norms they established, what protocol they followed, what leadership style prevailed).

Rather, it came down to *how* those team members interacted. Their success rose or fell on whether they were able to create "psychological safety," which Amy Edmondson defined as "a shared belief held by members of a team that the team is safe for interpersonal risk taking."[6] Another definition published by William Kahn back in 1990 in the *Academy of Management Journal* adds a bit more nuance by stating that it's "being able to show and employ one's self without fear of negative consequences of self-image, status or career."[7] No one wants to be embarrassed, punished, or thought less of for sharing ideas, revealing needs, or risking what would be perceived as failure.

Now, while we won't see the Three Requirements stated as blatantly (psychological safety is basically to groups what trust is to any two individuals), we can immediately see that to develop this outcome we have to be willing to "show and employ one's self" (Vulnerability), "without fear of negative consequences" (outcome of Positivity), and the only way we can create this "shared belief that the team is safe" is through past experience (what I'm calling Consistency). We will unpack this in more detail in Chapter 7 as we look at the research that will point us to how to make our workplaces most conducive for growth, but time and again, study after study, while different words are used, you'll see some version of these Three Requirements.

And, a last note about commonalities. It's not that they aren't important at all as much as they aren't enough unless those similarities lead us to practicing the Three Requirements. If both people being part of a minority group helps us talk more openly (Vulnerability), then yes, it helps. If both being in the same profession helps us spend more time together (Consistency), then yes, it helps. If both having a similar sense of humor helps us enjoy each other more (Positivity), then yes, it helps. In other words, it's not the commonality that bonds us, unless the commonality motivates us to see each other more frequently, open up more, or feel more accepted.

Every healthy relationship you have ever experienced has had these Three Requirements; and conversely, any relationship that doesn't feel meaningful, or isn't working, lacks at least one of these Three Requirements.

THE DEFINITION OF FRIENDSHIP

In the next chapter, I'm going to elucidate how these three dynamics interact and work together in every relationship, but let's first build our working definition of friendship now that we know what we're looking for in every relationship we establish.

When We Practice Vulnerability, We Feel Seen

Most obvious to our task here is that what we're craving when we seek out relationships is some degree of feeling connected. We want to be admired, respected, and appreciated. And not because we're broken and needy, but because we have an awesome capacity to give and receive love in this world. We're made for it. We thrive on it. Our survival has been dependent on it. Our longevity is linked to it. Our happiness is correlated to it.

But ultimately, we'll only be known as we allow ourselves to be revealed. Which is the root of Vulnerability. The more we let someone see us (assuming it's in conjunction with Positivity with responses such as affirmation, acceptance, and empathy) then the more loved we'll feel for who we are. Name the people who love us the most and we'll name the people who know us the best. But even if we wouldn't describe needing love from our coworkers, every single one of us wants to believe that those around us think we're "good enough," which hinges on feeling seen for who we are and what we contribute.

We aren't just Vulnerable for the sake of Vulnerability but because it leads to what matters most: feeling seen.

When We Practice Consistency, We Feel Safe

There are moments in life when we can feel seen by someone we'll only meet once, whether it be at some hotel bar, on an airplane, or during an intense event, but if we want a *relationship*, the interaction has to be repeated. Being in relationship with someone implies an ongoing connection, a thread that keeps us joined, a belief that we'll interact again. Consistency is the action of replicating time together. As we add up the hours, stir in memories, and practice connecting in a variety of ways we compound the opportunities for two people to feel known and seen. Time—the prioritizing of it in the present, the eventual building up of it that creates a history, and the belief that there's a shared future—is the vehicle that gives us safety in our Vulnerability.

Because more than simply tallying hours together, the more Consistency we have, the more we feel like we can anticipate how a person will behave in different situations. That leads to us trusting someone as a result of our experience with them. And the more we can anticipate, or predict, someone's response, the safer we feel. Lack of Consistency breeds feelings like "walking on eggshells," or "worrying about how they'll respond."

With people we don't know well, the expectation might only be, "I trust them to show up at this lunch we scheduled together"; with a boss who has mentored us, it might look more like, "I trust him to advocate on my behalf in that meeting"; and with our sister it might be, "I trust that if I needed her, she'd be on the next plane." Trust isn't all or nothing. Trust is selective, discriminatory, and established from past actions.

Consistency leads to familiarity. Familiarity leaves us feeling comfortable, relaxed, and safe.

When We Practice Positivity, We Feel Satisfied

But knowing your sister will get on the plane, your boss will advocate for you, or that your friend will show up at the agreed-upon time is one thing; whether we end up feeling happy, or good, is another. Yes, it still feels supportive to know you can count on them for those things, but does your lunch date keep looking at his phone every two minutes, does your boss now act like you owe her for the rest of your career, and does your sister show up ready to be medaled with martyr of the year? Feeling that trust based on our time together is one requirement, but we can't leave out Positivity!

Positivity is when we are left feeling good about that time together. We want to feel good about ourselves—our lives, our choices, our strengths, our contributions, our personality, our body, our way of doing things. We all want laughter, joy, pride, and awe. None of us are waking up on any given day hoping for more people to whine and complain to us, hoping we're left feeling insecure and wondering what they think of us, or boring us to death without laughter, curiosity, or interest.

While positive feelings are necessary in all healthy relationships, they are paramount to our friendships because these are the relationships we are entering by choice. And these good feelings are the engine for the other two requirements: we are more likely to be consistent with someone if our time together feels good, and we're more likely to tell our stories and share our thoughts and ideas if they respond in ways that feel good.

At the end of the day, a friendship needs to feel satisfying, which means it needs to feel good, leaving us feeling positive.

Forming a Definition Based on the Three Requirements

Based on the science of knowing that we can measure the health and depth of any relationship based on its Vulnerability, Consistency, and Positivity, a definition emerges that reflects what we're looking for when we are seeking out friendship:

A friendship is any relationship in which both people feel **seen** in a **safe** and **satisfying** way.

Of course, as we'll see in the next several chapters, there are varying levels of friendship, so what we want witnessed, or seen, by a friend we barely know on social media will appropriately look different to what we share with our bestest friend in the world, and what we want seen by our boss will look different than what we want seen by our romantic interest. But in all cases, we *do* want *something* to be noticed in a way that leaves us feeling good.

I can't wait to jump into the next chapter to show you how these three factors lead to all kinds of relationship wisdom, but for now just remember:

1. We feel **seen** as we practice **Vulnerability**,
2. We feel **safe** as we practice **Consistency**, and
3. We feel **satisfied** as we practice **Positivity**.

How Friendships Are Developed

The Frientimacy Triangle

Okay, so you're undoubtedly anxious to find out what this all means in practical ways to your work. And I promise you that every chapter from here on out will provide you with stories, tips, case studies, and research to support you whether you're a CEO looking to improve your employee engagement and retention, an entrepreneur thoughtfully thinking through your start-up culture, an HR specialist focused on employee development, a manager who longs to have a dynamic team, or someone who simply wants the time at work to suck less. But before we dive in too deep to specific applications, we need to understand how the Three Requirements work together.

I teach the Three Requirements on what I've long called the Frientimacy Triangle, and while I toyed with changing the name of it for you, my dear work-focused friends, I decided to stick with the name since, after all, you *are* still human even though you have a job. And humans need Frientimacy—the intimacy of friends, or more specifically, intimacy that has nothing to do with sex.

"Wait, what?" I hear your protests from here: "I understand the Three Requirements of relationships, but I definitely don't want that Frientimacy with everyone at work."

Fair enough. All the more reason to keep that word in there—showcasing what's possible at the deepest end of a few of our relationships—to both remind us that we need to be building that level of relationships in our lives *somewhere* if not at work, and to help us keep healthy expectations of what most of our work relationships won't be, even if at times we feel closer to people whom we see every day at work.

As we will see in a variety of ways through this book, and in really clear terms in Chapter 8, there are many shades of relationship between nonfriend and Frientimacy. But you gotta know both ends of the spectrum to better understand the options in the middle! To calm your beating little heart down, though, let me assure you that most of this book isn't about Frientimacy. (If you're interested in improving some of your friendships and leaning into deeper intimacy, read my book *Frientimacy: How to Deepen Friendships for Lifelong Health and Happiness*.)

This book is about friendship in the broadest of terms, so that we know how to develop more meaningful *friendships* with a few and how to be *friendlier* to everyone else.

HOW THE FRIENTIMACY TRIANGLE DEVELOPS RELATIONSHIPS

We've established that we need Positivity, Consistency, and Vulnerability in every relationship. To illustrate how those work together, I've placed them on a Triangle with Positivity at the base, and Consistency and Vulnerability as the two arms that stretch up to eventually meet at the peak.

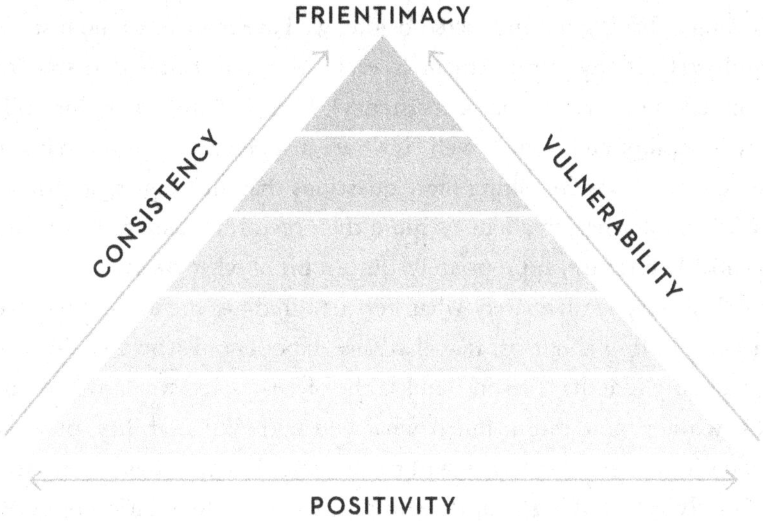

In a nutshell, this is how it works: every single relationship you have starts at the bottom of the Triangle on a foundation of Positivity; some of them eventually move up the Triangle as we implement increased amounts of Consistency and Vulnerability; and a few will reach the top where the highest levels of Positivity, Consistency, and Vulnerability are practiced between two people.

Let me walk you through it.

1. Every relationship starts with Positivity at the bottom of the Triangle.

No matter how much we initially like someone, how much chemistry or respect we feel, or how many obvious things we have in common—every single relationship starts at the bottom of the Triangle—on a foundation of Positivity, with low levels of Consistency and Vulnerability.

What that means is that ideally there are enough positive feelings (produced perhaps from how they looked us in the eye, smiled, complimented something about us, showed curiosity in us, and generally left us feeling good) that we want to lean in, repeat the experience, or get to know them better. At this point, along the bottom of the

Triangle, having not interacted before, we have no pattern, no history, and little, if any, commitment to each other (all things that start to happen as we increase our Consistency). Furthermore, our Vulnerability is appropriately low, as well, as we are just beginning to get to know each other. So we're asking more questions than making assumptions, sharing information about us more than revealing deep feelings, and probably filtering, appropriately, quite a bit of what we say.

Positivity is ultimately what gets us hired—someone had to have a good feeling about us; it's what's we experienced when we say "we just really like that person," and as the often-quoted wisdom reminds us, while people might forget what you said (Vulnerability) or what you did (Consistency), they will never forget how you made them feel (Positivity). Leaving people feeling good is the foundation of every relationship and will be the determining factor for whether people want to increase their Consistency and Vulnerability with us.

There is definitely a big difference between those with whom we're *friendly* versus those with whom we're *friends*, but underneath both of them is a foundation of kindness, respect, and goodwill. Therefore, whether we are friendly to them—those complaining customers, high-maintenance clients, or irritating teammates—is not up for debate. At the end of the day, our goal is to be in as many satisfying relationships and enjoyable relational moments as possible—which means we'll do what we can to increase our chances, and theirs, of feeling good. In more practical terms, the moral of the story is: be kind to everyone.

2. The healthiest relationships develop in an escalating and incremental way up the Triangle as we practice the behaviors of friendship.

Social studies continue to reveal that we can bond nearly any two people or group of people by slowly, but surely, increasing our experience of these Three Requirements. As our Consistency slowly increases—with each time we see each other, how frequently we interact, and how long we've known each other—so, too, should our Vulnerability

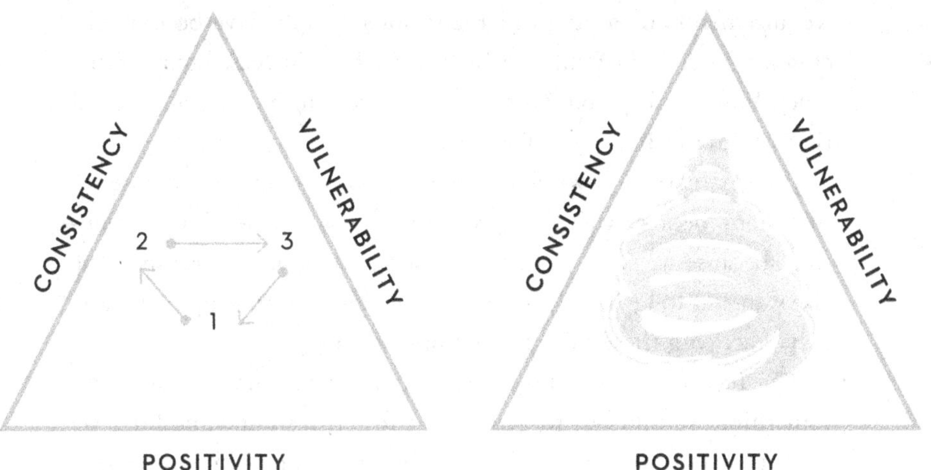

incrementally increase. And every time our Vulnerability increases, as we reveal something else about ourselves—asking for something that would help us do our jobs better, admitting when we don't know something, or sharing a far-fetched solution to a problem—so, too, should our experience of Positivity then increase—as they respond with words of resonance, empathy, encouragement, and support.

Therefore, these three factors should continue to spiral upwards: add a bit of sharing, follow it up with receiving some affirmation or something that says thanks for taking that risk, and then we repeat. If the loop gets broken—either because we never took the risk to be seen, or because the response left us feeling bad—we're less likely to continue to build a healthy relationship and we'll get stuck somewhere far lower on the Triangle than might serve us or our company's mission.

Our relationships become stronger the more we perform actions that leave both people feeling seen in a safer and more satisfying way.

3. Only a few relationships develop to the Top of the Triangle into Frientimacy—friendship intimacy.

The more we practice these Three Requirements, the stronger our relationship becomes. All of our relationships have these Three

Requirements in varying order, and some people have become our closest friends and confidantes because we have increased our Consistency, Vulnerability, and Positivity over time, which eventually moved them up to the Top of the Triangle.

It bears repeating: we aren't moving someone up just because we like them, because we've entered into a formal mentorship relationship, because we want to be friends with them, or because someone else wants us to be friends—we can only move someone up by repeatedly practicing these three relationship actions.

The Top of the Triangle emphasizes that friendship intimacy isn't something we find but something we foster; it's not something we simply choose but something we create; not something we bestow on someone as though it's a job opening we're trying to fill but rather something we work on together to accomplish. The Top of the Triangle is reserved for the people we trust implicitly (the result of high Consistency), feel we can tell anything to (the result of high Vulnerability), and with whom we feel the most loved (the result of high Positivity). While there are plenty of stories of work colleagues developing to this level, it isn't the goal for most of us in most of our relationships.

4. Most relationships, therefore, are somewhere in the middle of the Triangle. Appropriately so.

For most of our relationships, it's helpful to have a visual reminder that there is a vast difference between the bulk of the friendships we're developing at work and those select few you'd develop to the pinnacle of Frientimacy.

Truth be told, we will undoubtedly only experience Frientimacy—the highest level of Vulnerability, Consistency, and Positivity—with a handful of people at any given stage of our lives—in part because few of us have that kind of time and emotional bandwidth to foster that many relationships (most of us report greatest happiness with anywhere between three to five close friends), but also because we understand on some important level that not every relationship needs to be that close in order to still be healthy, significant, meaningful, or helpful. This isn't an all-or-nothing game. It's not best friend or bust. Relationships are valuable, no matter where they reside.

One of the most important things we can remind our brains is that we can be friends with people, even somewhat close friends in a particular area, without needing them to become our best friends at the Top of the Triangle. Research shows that we're happiest if we have friends at the places we frequent. Whether that be places of religious worship, our kids' school, at that networking association, or in our office, we feel like we belong and have support if we can gravitate to friends in each setting.

We'll get into this more, but even when someone says they have a "best friend at work," chances are high that their Vulnerability is probably more focused on certain subjects and their Consistency is often still completely centered upon their work schedules matching up, so it's helpful to remember that even when we feel super close to someone because we see them every day and share day-to-day life stories with them, that isn't automatically the same as what we might mean when we say "Frientimacy." Again, not to say it can't develop into that, but it is to say that it's completely okay to have "best friends at work" and understand what that is, and what that isn't.

What we need to know for now is that not every friendship needs to be a 100 percent on all Three Requirements to be valuable in our lives—a bunch of coworkers, a mastermind of other entrepreneurs, or an online support group for writers and artists who are all in the 40–60 percent range, so to speak, are great! Not everyone needs to be, or even can be, at the top of our Triangle. Our goal is simply to make sure that we have as much Positivity as possible, healthy expectations that reflect the level of our Consistency, or commitment, and appropriate matching of our Vulnerability. I'll unpack this more, in great detail, in Chapter 8.

5. *Any relationship that doesn't feel as good as we want it to is because at least one of these requirements is lacking.*

We have never developed a meaningful relationship without these Three Requirements being present; and conversely, any relationship that isn't feeling healthy is because at least one of these Three Requirements is lacking. Name any relationship in your life and you can probably pretty quickly start to identify which one of these would make the biggest difference to each friendship.

For one relationship, it might have high Positivity and high Consistency—meaning you enjoy them and see them regularly, but without high Vulnerability, they will remain someone fun to do things with, but not someone you feel close to.

For another relationship, you might have high Vulnerability and high Positivity—meaning you shared an amazing time together when you both really felt seen and appreciated, but if you never repeated the experience, or saw them again (Consistency) then you won't ultimately feel supported by that person.

For another relationship, you might have high Vulnerability and high Consistency—meaning you both tell each other everything and interact regularly, but without high Positivity, you'll feel more drained and weary than energized by that relationship.

One last example: often we recognize in some of our friendships that our Vulnerability and Consistency are out of balance—either that we have known someone forever and see them all the time (high Consistency) but we're still not opening up to them (low Vulnerability), or that we might barely know someone (low Consistency) and yet we're in the habit of oversharing and thinking that everyone we meet is our new best friend (high Vulnerability). In both cases, the awareness invites us to practice more healthy sharing that is reflected by the *actual* level of relationship we've developed.

Most of our relationships aren't missing one ingredient completely, but we can probably name exactly which one would make that relationship feel better if we were to increase it.

6. Our expectations of the relationship should be based on the level of relationship that has been practiced thus far.

One of my favorite things about reminding our brains that relationships have to be developed, and that not all relationships are developed to the same height on the Triangle, is that it invites us to shift our expectations to accurately reflect the relationship that has been developed. Not the relationship we wish we had. Not the relationship we need. Not the relationship we both said we wanted. Nope. Our expectations have to be congruent with the relationship that is a result of how much Consistency, Vulnerability, and Positivity have already been practiced.

In fact, most relationships that feel fraught with disappointment, resentment, or hurt feelings usually come down to one thing: mismatched expectations for the level of relationship developed.

Let me give some quick examples from some specific situations that jump to my mind. Molly was heartbroken six months after leaving her last job because her best friends from that office hadn't called or initiated getting together since her departure. "I guess they weren't good friends, after all," she said with judgment and despair. After a bit of probing, I discovered that all of their previous Consistency had happened at work. They had no practice in spending time together on weekends, talking on the phone, or grabbing dinner together with their spouses. I gently helped her see that she had stepped out of the only structure those friendships knew, and naturally, the friendships had only two choices: 1) wither from lack of consistent interaction, or 2) learn new ways of initiating, inviting, and scheduling. It wasn't that those women who hadn't called weren't good friends, or that their shared friendships hadn't been meaningful and healthy for what they were, but Molly had pulled the rug out on their only way of experiencing Consistency together and hadn't shifted her expectations accordingly.

Molly's story is more common than not. For those of you who fear that you will face the same challenges, I have a whole bonus chapter available at thebusinessoffriendship.com on how to transition these friendships, if you want!

Another example of how hurt we can be when our expectations aren't in alignment with our actual relationships is illustrated by Dave. He describes his construction work friends to me as his best friends. In fact, he'd say they are his only friends since he doesn't really have anyone he hangs out with outside of work. They joke a lot during breaks, share high levels of pride over finished jobs, competitively play *Words with Friends* as they eat their lunches, and frequently grab beers together after work. But his dad recently died after a long and exhausting illness, and he felt betrayed that none of his best friends were really "there" for him. He acknowledged that two or three of them had come to the funeral, but beyond that, no one had asked him much about it or offered to help in any way. He was licking his wounds and wondering, "What's the point of having friends if not for those moments in life?" Indeed, I agreed. And I ache with him that they weren't there in the way he wanted. But, again, this is a perfect example of how we are at risk of often bestowing the title, and expectations, of "best friends" without really having practiced all Three Requirements to warrant that level of relationship. Because Dave didn't have anyone at the top of his Triangle, he made the innocent mistake of assuming that the people he felt closest to were automatically up there. But truthfully, they were probably only about 30–40 percent of the way up. And we can't expect friends down there—ones that hardly spent time together outside of their work schedules and had little history of sharing their pain, processing their feelings, or showing up to support each other—to act like they are on the Top of the Triangle when they aren't.

Our relational happiness comes down to alignment—our ability to make sure that the relationships we want are the ones we're practicing, and conversely, to make sure our expectations match what is.

The beautiful reality is that most people are not maliciously trying to hurt us. So much of our disappointment and frustration can serve as an invitation to inquire, "If I were really honest, what is the relationship that has been developed and practiced so far?" And then, more importantly, "If I want it to be more meaningful, what can I do to help move us closer to what I ultimately want?" To foster the friendships they wanted, Molly would need to initiate rebuilding the Consistency with her friends that she missed, and Dave would need to practice increasing the Vulnerability he ultimately wanted.

7. While we can't change people, we can always change the relationship we have with them.

Our relationships don't "just happen" to us. As we become more competent in practicing these skills, we see the role we have in cocreating every relationship in our lives. You've likely developed and ended some relationships without awareness or intention, but you've never developed any relationship without increasing these three factors or ended any relationship without decreasing these three factors.

Relationship 101 reminds us that in any given relationship we have three entities:

1. Person 1/Me
2. Person 2/the Other
3. The Relationship

While we can't change the other, we can change ourselves and how we show up and respond to the other, which in turn changes the relationship. And by changing the relationship we, at minimum, invite the other to choose a different response, which then sometimes changes the other as they get the chance to practice new responses. But at the very least, for our purposes: ultimately, we don't need *the other* to change, as much as we need *our interaction with that person* to feel better.

This is crucial to remind our brains because when we feel frustrated or disappointed in a relationship, our initial, albeit mistaken, tendency is to overattribute the cause of someone's behavior to who they are, instead of seeing the circumstances that invoked their response.

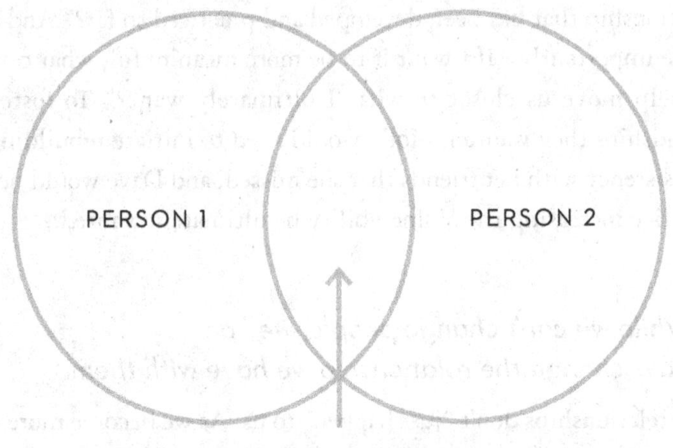

Psychology calls it fundamental attribution error, but it basically means that when we mess up we are quick to justify and explain it (and ultimately believe that as long as our motivations were good then that's what matters most). But with others, we aren't as gracious to assume their motivations were good, or that they did the best they could in the circumstances.

As we challenge ourselves to pay greater attention to the circumstances in our relationship with them—the questions we ask, the events we plan, the things we share, the affirmation we give or withhold—it's often the case that we can repair the relationship, deepen the relationship, or at the very least change our expectations of the relationship.

For example, if we have a coworker who always complains, vents, and sees the worst of things, we might be tempted to label her as negative and assume that the only way to raise the Positivity in our relationship is for *her* to change. But because we're basically relationship rock stars who are out to improve our corner of the world, we can brainstorm how we might better navigate the conversation in such a way that leaves our relationship/interaction feeling better, which then increases the odds that both people leave feeling better.

- If we validate her feelings (for example, "oh, that does sound frustrating!") instead of dismissing them as nothing—does she respond differently when she feels heard?
- If we gently invite her to express gratitude (for example, "I know you've been unhappy in your role for a while, but remind me again what parts of it you do like?") instead of just pumping her up with false encouragement—does she respond differently when we ask her a reflective question?
- If we affirm specific things we see in her (for example, "I know that situation is frustrating, but can I just say how impressed I am that you've continued to support his project even though you're not pleased with how it's unfolding!") instead of giving advice—does she respond differently when she feels recognized?

We can improve the relationships around us.

That's not the same as saying we are at fault for how things are. Rather it acknowledges that we are the ones committed to being as happy and healthy as we can be. We are the ones called to teach, model, and inspire the relationships that this world needs. Besides, we aren't necessarily increasing our Positivity in a relationship for *their* sake or because they "deserve" it but because *we* want to enjoy our time at work as much as possible, alleviate stress around us, create better products and services, and be as available to contribute our best selves as possible!

It's in self-interest that we experiment with changing the circumstances of our interactions. We choose to remain clear that while we're not able to change the other, we are always building our relational muscles and increasing our capacity for better relationships. Ergo, we win no matter what. When we look at how we can increase the Three Requirements in our relationships, we do so knowing that everything we give to a relationship is also giving to ourselves.

But even though it's never a waste to try to improve a relationship, it's worth noting here that sometimes relationships need to decrease more than they need to increase. In Chapter 9, on dealing with coworkers who annoy us, I will walk us through how to back a relationship down to a level that better reflects the relationship that feels safest to us. Not every relationship can be repaired, nor does "fixing" it mean that we still have to be close or that we trust them in all areas. While keeping the focus of this chapter on how relationships work, for now tuck away the truth that we'll revisit in detail: relationships not only move up this Triangle, they also move down it.

In every relationship, while we can't wave a magic wand over the other person and make them dance to our song, we can change the music. In an ideal world, we fix and repair relationships so both people feel more seen in a safe and satisfying way. When that doesn't always work, at least we've practiced becoming a better dancer, which will benefit all our other relationships.

A SUMMARY OF HOW RELATIONSHIPS WORK

I wish we were in a workshop so I could look you in the eyes and ask, "Does all of this make sense? Are you with me still? Is this helpful?"

For now, because we have these pages between us, I'm going to have to assume you'll respond like the thousands of other people I have taught, which means hopefully you're nodding your heads and already seeing some of your relationships differently. Some of you are undoubtedly nodding more enthusiastically than others, as a bunch of your relationships are starting to really make sense to you. I'm excited for you!

Most of you are still taking it in, perhaps feeling a bit incredulous that you're only just now hearing all of this at this age in life: "Why have I never been taught this before? This would have been helpful to know back at my last job!" Indeed, it would have. Isn't it amazing that *everything* in life is built on our relationships and yet few of us have ever taken a single class on the subject? That we know it now always leaves me grateful; it reminds me to be gentle on all of those we're interacting with who still don't know what they don't know.

And undoubtedly there are several of you now who have more questions than answers, and hopefully you have some healthy skepticism about what this actually looks like in real life, in the world of your work. I, for one, am eager to get to all of that and can only hope that by the time you finish this book you feel like all your questions have been answered. (And if not, you're welcome to write me! Or, check out my YouTube channel where I may have covered it!)

But before we jump into application in our next chapter, humor the teacher in me and let's review one more time what we've learned:

1. Every relationship starts at the bottom of the Triangle, with a foundation of Positivity.
2. The healthiest relationships develop in an escalating, and incremental, way up the Triangle as we increase Consistency and Vulnerability.
3. Only a few relationships develop to the Top of the Triangle into Frientimacy—friendship intimacy. They get there as a result of having practiced the highest of Positivity, Consistency, and Vulnerability.
4. Most relationships, therefore, are somewhere in the middle of the Triangle. Appropriately so.
5. Any relationship that doesn't feel as good as we want is because at least one of these requirements is lacking.
6. Our expectations of the relationship should be based on the level of relationship that has been practiced thus far.
7. While we can't change people, we can always change the relationship we have with them.

Now let's go make these truths work for us and our relationships by diving deeper into each of the Three Requirements, starting with Positivity.

5

How to Develop Relationships at Work That Are Positive

What we want more than anything in life is to be satisfied, to feel good, to be happy. We will gravitate to the activities, people, and places that increase that feeling; and conversely, we'll withdraw or avoid the activities, people, and places that decrease that feeling. We've all chosen jobs hoping they would lead to more of this, and many of us have left jobs upon the realization that we were feeling anything but that.

If our workplace is happy, we enjoy our work more, are more engaged in our collective success, feel more creative, accomplish more, exhibit more self-confidence, and are more likely to support each other. That's a lot of mores. But just as significant is what there is less of too: less turnover, less burnout, less conflict, less sickness and injury, less depression, and less stress.

And let's face it, we live in a stressed-out time. It's a vicious cycle that the more stressed we are, the lonelier we seem, and the more depressed we'll feel—and the more depressed we feel, the less likely we are to get our social needs met, which in turn, you guessed it, escalates our stress. The spiral is real.

- In a career survey, 80 percent of us rank our stress as a 7 or higher on a 10-point scale.[1]
- Close to 50 percent of us say that we are often, or always, exhausted due to our work. (And it's not only a 32 percent increase from two decades ago, but it's steadily increasing each year.)[2]
- Eight out of ten of us have cried at work, with almost half of us crying because of our bosses and coworkers. Almost one in ten of us cries weekly, and one in twenty of us reports crying daily.[3]
- Sixty-four percent of us have nightmares about work[4] and 34 percent of us report difficulty sleeping from our job stress.[5]
- And even if we're not the stressed-out ones, 14 percent of our coworkers admitted to feeling like "striking a coworker in the past year," 42 percent report that yelling and verbal abuse is common, and 25 percent of our colleagues have felt like screaming or shouting, so we're not totally unaffected.[6]

I could go on, but we hardly need stats to tell us all of this.

None of us head off to work hoping our coworkers are extra whiny, gossipy, manipulative, or sullen today. We don't want to return home needing to detox from the frustrations of our boss or dripping from the polite smiles of people we barely know. Not a single one of us lies in bed at night wishing for a more negative and draining workplace. At the end of the day, if asked if we want more positive interactions at work, we'd all raise our hands. I'll bet even the very people whom we think are ruining our particular workplace with their incessant complaining, micromanaging, or demeaning behaviors say they want to work in a positive environment too.

None of us are waiting for one more stat to tell us we prefer to feel good and enjoy each other. In fact, for more than 75 percent of the teams who have taken the *Healthy Team Relationship Assessment*, Positivity is consistently the lowest score of the Three Relationship Requirements. We need more of it. We talk a lot about positive culture, but culture is nothing if it's not relationships. If we want to be happy at work, we have to be happy with the people we work alongside.

For our sake—because we can't sit and wait for our boss to make us happy, nor satisfy ourselves for long with just pointing to whom we think is to blame for our unhappiness—we will ask, "What can I do to contribute more Positivity around here?"

POSITIVITY IS DEVELOPED

At **the bottom of the Triangle**, we don't yet feel completely satisfied as we don't yet have a history of validation, empathy, shared fun, and expressed love, but we can still aim for being friendly and kind. We don't need to like them, believe we'll ever see them again, or admire them—but our *kind actions* will convey that we honor them as people.

The goal of Positivity is to leave both people feeling good about having interacted so that we might want to continue to practice Consistency and Vulnerability with each other. Research has shown that, regardless of our culture or context, we judge a new person on two primary factors: warmth and competency.

But guess which one comes first? Warmth before competency! Throughout history, our survival was dependent first upon our ability to decide who was an ally or enemy. We are wired to instantly assess whether someone is warm, nice, and friendly. The second factor, competency, builds over time as we assess the person's skills and effectiveness, which helps us then determine how helpful as an ally, or dangerous as an enemy, the person could prove to be.[7] Before we can

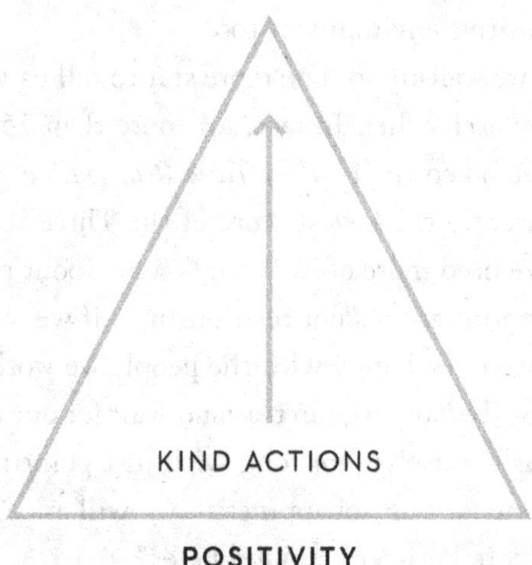

build any strong collaboration or relationship with others—we have to feel the warmth and believe that we each want to be allies. It's our job to give this, not just look to receive it. In fact, the healthiest among us will be quick to offer it, whether we get it in return or not. We know that it's good business, and good humanity, to be kind everywhere we go.

We must find a baseline on which we offer up kind actions and friendliness to everyone. Then, with those who matter to us, we can hopefully move those relationships up the Triangle as we practice building on our kind actions by adding to the rewards we feel in this relationship: more laughter, more expressed gratitude, more meaningful compliments, and more vocalized support.

At the Top of the Triangle we experience *complete acceptance* where we feel more confident that we love each other, more comfortable demonstrating that, and more willing to personalize the way we care for each other based on what the other needs. Ideally, we don't need to doubt what the other thinks about us, hesitate to express our adoration, or fear how they'll respond to something we share because we feel secure commitment (highest level of Consistency) and meaningful transparency (highest level of Vulnerability).

HOW TO DEVELOP POSITIVITY

The number one requirement of healthy relationships is that they leave us feeling good, most of the time. We seek out relationships that feel rewarding to us, with people we enjoy, and with whom we have fun. At the base of our Triangle, we start with Positivity—the experience of feeling more positive about ourselves, and our lives, for having interacted.

Positivity is positive emotions.

To be clear what Positivity is, it's also important to be clear what it isn't. Positivity does not mean that we need to be a more positive person or say only positive things. It doesn't mean trying to cheer people up, pretending to like everything, or saying yes to everyone. It doesn't stipulate that we don't go through hard things, struggle with depression, or get angry. It doesn't ask us to put on a fake brave face, force us to smile insincerely, or give us an excuse to avoid tough conversations. It doesn't mean we can't vent, whine, or complain. It doesn't indicate that we don't work hard, have deadlines, or vehemently disagree with each other.

What Positivity does mean is that, over time and along the way, we feel positive emotions toward each other. Whether we're measuring Positivity in our own life, in a specific relationship, or on our team—what we're looking for are more positive emotions than negative emotions.

Feeling more positive emotions is what fosters our happiness. Dr. Barbara Fredrickson, who has made it her life work to study positive emotions and is the author of the book *Positivity*, says that in her research the ten most common emotions that lead to Positivity are joy, gratitude, serenity, interest, hope, pride, amusement, inspiration, awe, and love.[8] Who among us wouldn't want our team feeling more *inspired*? Our clients feeling more *grateful*? Or ourselves feeling more *pride* for the valuable contributions we're making? For our purposes, we can add to the list or even use different words to describe the result of Positivity. Words I hear often from teams when I ask them to name what feelings they most want at work also include curiosity, empathy, confidence, admiration, respect, contentment, enjoyment, appreciation, and excitement. Our happiness is correlated with the quantifying of our positive emotions.

And while we want to feel as many emotions from the above list as possible, there are two emotions that I want to especially call out, as I've never seen a healthy team exist without these two core social emotions.

Empathy is connecting with someone's emotions about an experience they're going through in a way that leaves them feeling seen and validated. It's the response we are looking for most of the time when we tell stories, complain, or celebrate because we want to feel like they *get it,* that they see our experience from our perspective. When someone can mirror back our emotions and validate them, we not only feel more normal because we don't feel judged, but we also feel more connected to them. The powerful thing is that empathy isn't about having the right answers, fixing the problem, cheering someone up, or agreeing with them—it's simply the ability to sit for a moment in *their* feeling and communicate, "You're not alone; I'm with you." When we unpack Vulnerability in Chapter 7, we'll see that few people will want to practice Vulnerability with us if we can't learn to validate people's feelings in a way that leaves them feeling valued. And the good news is that the more we practice these skills the better, for as Maria Ross, the author of *The Empathy Edge,* assures us, empathy has a "direct impact on everything from customer loyalty to innovation to profits."[9]

Appreciation is gratitude directed at someone. We know that gratitude is perhaps the most powerful emotion that can rewire our brains and change our lives, so imagine how powerful it is when we can direct that thanks to someone else. Feeling recognized for what we contribute, and who we are, fosters contentment, loyalty, and confidence and leads to improved productivity, morale, and engagement.

The more we feel seen and appreciated, the less likely we are to suffer from jealousy, complaining, entitlement, and fear of favoritism. Countless studies have been conducted that remind us that feeling appreciated is one of the top engagement factors. Unfortunately, about 40 percent of us don't feel our organizations prioritize recognizing our contributions even though 82 percent of us would prefer that over a gift or bonus.[10] And while we collectively want it most from our managers, if our coworkers are involved in our recognition—say with a milestone anniversary celebration—our engagement increases 21 percent more than if the reward just came from the company.[11] We want to know we're appreciated so much so that 69 percent of us say we'd work harder if we felt our efforts were better recognized.[12] And the best news is that it leads to reciprocity, which means it has a contagious element to it—we can be the ones who appreciate others knowing it will eventually lead to an increase in our receiving of it. When we unpack Consistency in the next chapter, we'll better understand how much more likely we are to want to spend more time around people who express their appreciation of us.

Positivity is the result of our actions.

What produces these positive emotions? They are a bodily response to actions or words that we, or others, trigger with our actions.

In other words, when we want our team to feel more of one of those emotions, let's say *hope*, we unfortunately can't just wave a magic wand or insist they feel hopeful. Rather we ask, "What could I do that might help us feel more hopeful right now?" And then we pursue one of those actions. We can increase the quantity of times we, and those around us, feel these positive emotions by the actions we set into motion.

We don't just automatically feel *enjoyment* together; rather, it's the result of us having fun together on a team retreat, laughing over a shared joke during a meeting, or feeling like our engaging conversation was stimulating and mutually interesting.

When we feel insecure about a new assignment, we can't just insist on feeling *confidence*. But we might increase it by asking our manager why they chose us for this particular project and what they think we can bring to the challenge, practicing certain postures or expressions that science shows boost that emotion, or picking one action we do feel confident getting started with to help us accomplish a small win on our way to the bigger goal. Actions produce emotions.

Kayla, a shift supervisor for a coffee shop, wasn't impressed with how her manager left everyone feeling ignored, so she implemented two new rituals to increase *gratitude* and *appreciation* on each shift she managed: 1) starting every shift with all workers sharing one good thing going on in their personal life—something they were grateful for or something they enjoyed recently, and 2) ending every shift with each person expressing something good from that shift—thanks to a colleague or a rewarding moment with a customer.

Dan, a dentist with a team of eight employees, loved being generous by bringing in occasional treats or hosting fun team gatherings around his pool for their families, but he also wanted to help his office staff and dental hygienists practice more *generosity* with each other. Now, every quarter, he gives them each an envelope with three small gift cards in them for the purpose of them gifting those to each other. They gift them, at their choosing, during staff meetings so that the whole team gets a boost of Positivity hearing what prompted the gifting.

Unfortunately, on the *Healthy Team Relationship Assessment,* one of the lowest scoring statements consistently is: "We intentionally spend time together in ways that promote amusement, awe, hope, joy, interest, or inspiration." Too few of us are feeling it. And while it's easy to name things we wish our managers would do for us, I can assure you, having worked with so many teams, that those without the title can be just as impactful, if not more so. For us to find the right place in a meeting to raise our hand and praise a coworker for something we saw shifts the collective DNA. We can organize a pool party, or a potluck, or a happy hour for our team just as easily as our boss can. Plus, it's not just us who wants Positivity from our leaders; they need it from us too. What are we doing to show our appreciation to them? Do we ever pitch in and surprise them with generosity? Do we take the time to praise them in front of their supervisors or the team? Do we stop by their office and ask, "Is there any way I can support you better right now?"

Reminding ourselves that we can boost Positivity in offices, classrooms, warehouses, stores, and video conferences around the world reminds us that we are not victims who have no say in whether we feel the feelings we want to feel. Without a doubt, really disappointing, painful, and stressful things happen that cannot be stopped, prevented, or minimized; but as cliché as it sounds, we still have choices about how we want to respond to increase the chances of us, and others, feeling more Positivity at the end of the crisis and throughout the situation. We can invite, influence, prompt, invoke, motivate, and inspire those around us as we take the time to learn more about what helps each of us feel more positive emotions.

Positivity is the goal in every relationship.

Whether we want more friends, or simply a less toxic work environment, the most important thing we can do is pay attention to how people feel after they've spent time with us. Most of us are well attuned to how *we* feel after an interaction, but can we honestly say, "I brought more joy to their life today"? It's the oft-repeated "Focus more on being interested than in being interesting." Or, for many of us, it's the call to worry less about impressing everyone and instead be someone looking for the impressive in others.

Conversely, some of us have become so closed, gruff, or annoyed that we've convinced ourselves that no one else is worth our time and energy. We have devalued others so much in our mind, and justified it, that we've concluded that our treatment of them is defensible. We think *they* are the problem when it may very well be that *we* are contributing to the negativity just as much as they are.

Others of us may be hiding our lack of kindness behind a mask of false authenticity. We say things like, "What they see is what they get," "I shouldn't have to change for others," "It's okay that not everyone likes me," or "I don't want to be a kiss-ass like everyone else." Similar to the phrase *false humility*—sounding but not being humble—these phrases aren't healthy authenticity as much as they are veneers built for self-protection. While there's a shred of truth to many of those statements, if we're using them as weapons for distancing ourselves, then we've swallowed the lie that our true selves aren't kind, curious, and loving.

We all have different personalities and strengths so what we say and how we do it will vary, but our job description, no matter our title, is to leave people feeling better about themselves, or their lives, for having interacted with us. Obviously, some of our interactions are only moments long, or are very stressful, and yet our goal is, at minimum, to always show kindness.

Unlike Consistency and Vulnerability, which we might give to some and not others, Positivity—the desire to leave people feeling something positive—is something we give to everyone. We don't withhold it, dole it out only to the deserving, or offer it only when we like someone. My rule is that we can be friendly to everyone but then be more discerning about with whom we choose to build a friendship.

Think of the brash coworker whom we can barely stand to be around. Our every response, for good or for bad, is putting something into the bank account of that relationship. Every eye roll, every short answer, every interruption, every dodge to walk as far away from them as possible, every silent judgment—it's only contributing to the unhealthy relationship. We're not blameless just because we think they're annoying. Our moods and actions are contagious. We might feel righteous, defensive, justified—but our negative response is hurting everyone. What would change if we believed that everyone deserved to be treated with the bare minimum of positive friendly actions? What might happen if we chose to smile with our eyes, not just that curt fake smile? What might shift if we found something to affirm? What might change if we asked them more questions about their life so we could see their humanity and better empathize with them? What might we do differently if we believed this person was deserving and worthy of our kind actions?

Positivity must be higher than negativity.

There have been a lot of fascinating studies over the years inquiring how much Positivity we need—whether it be in our own lives, in our marriages, or on our teams. The researchers all vary in how they conduct their research, what exactly they're measuring, and what ratio they end up saying is the "tipping point" of how much Positivity we need for maximum success.

I often quote John Gottman's work, as he is world renowned for his research in relationships. In studying relationships, marriages specifically, his research showed that happy and successful relationships had at least five positive interactions for every negative interaction. By sharp contrast, failed marriages had less than a one-to-one ratio.

Other ratios I've seen as researchers study high-performing teams, mental health, and all variation of success have ranged between three-to-one and six-to-one. But there are two things they all agree on, and the first one is this: we need far more Positivity than negativity.

We have a *negativity bias*, which is the term scientists use to explain why the intensity of bad is felt stronger than the intensity of good. One bad review or criticism isn't made up with one rave review or praise. Someone rolling their eyes at something we said during a meeting isn't offset by them coming up and joking with us afterward. A customer yelling at us isn't equaled out by them smiling once at us before they leave.

Whether we need three, five, or six times more Positivity might be under some debate, but what is clear is that if we want high performance and happiness then the positive emotions need to far outweigh the negativity. By quite a bit, actually. Not even twice as much Positivity will put us at the lowest of the range. Think of it as a bank account in which we need five deposits of Positivity for every withdrawal of negativity.

The *frequency* of our positive emotions matters more to our end results than the *intensity* of any one negative emotion. To keep it practical, that means for every negative emotion we experience with our manager, a direct report, or a sales rep—to keep the relationship healthy we would want to look for ways to offset that with about five positive interactions. Examples are unlimited and would obviously be informed by how significant the relationship is and how much time we have had, or do have, together but a few might include: an apology, a willingness to find common ground, expressed appreciation for something specific, warm body language, validating their perspective, asking what we can do to make it right between us, or agreeing to go do something fun together.

Important to note, for our own personal Positivity, is that even if we can't get every relationship above that ratio, we can still strive to have our relationships in general above that ratio. In other words, one customer berating us probably isn't the place where we'll end up feeling positive. But we can still outweigh that interaction with an empathetic look from someone who overheard the interaction, validation from a supervisor that we handled it well, a joke from a coworker that lets off some steam, our own deep breath resulting in some peace, and a smile from our next customer. One can quickly see, however, that if someone we interact with frequently is constantly bringing the team down just how hard it can be to neutralize that barrage.

Think of the airline customer service representative who, while scrambling to rebook unhappy customers, can still apologize, show empathy, and give hope: "I am so sorry. I know this is so frustrating. I'm going to do what I can to get you home as soon as possible!" And, we know, from science, that should she still be able to throw a few more positive feelings into that interaction—free dinner voucher, a kind tone, rebooking on the next flight—chances are high that the customer will walk away feeling good, even though they were still delayed.

Leah, a social activist with a community organizing nonprofit, took this ratio to heart as she realized she was coming home feeling defeated most days from the overwhelming nature of her work. The next morning, she started a new channel in the collaboration software her organization uses and titled it "Things That Give Us Hope." She encouraged everyone to add in anything they wanted to the conversation, so it was available anytime anyone needed a boost.

The more negative, or stressful, our jobs are—the more we have to diligently ask ourselves: What can I do to interject as many positive emotions as possible into my work experience?

Positivity doesn't mean no negativity, but we can reduce it.

The second thing that all the research agrees on is this: every ratio includes negativity. Fortunately, no one has concluded that to be happy, high performing, and successful we need only positive emotions. The goal isn't even to strive for it! And therefore, your expectations should be such that you aren't surprised, shocked, or disappointed when the negative does show up.

Because show up it does. As you already know. Even if you and all your colleagues were the most mature, highly emotionally intelligent people on the face of the earth who never got defensive, took things personally, got annoyed with each other, or argued—we still have stressors in our relationships such as disappointing sales numbers, untenable deadlines, late shipments, or someone getting sick. We simply, and obviously, can't create an organizational dynamic that doesn't include negativity in some way or another. We will inevitably disappoint each other, irritate each other, and judge each other harshly for doing something differently than how we would have.

There's a strong case to be made for how negativity is important and crucial to our success. Feeling guilt after messing up, sadness after failing, or frustration after disappointment is part of being mentally healthy and can help us make better decisions. Disagreeing can lead to better outcomes, products, and ideas. Dealing with low resources, a tight deadline, or an impossible request may lead to greater creativity or surprise success. Crisis and fear can foster empathy and bring us closer to each other.

But often there really is no faster, or more effective, way to get that positivity to negativity ratio in balance than to decrease whatever negativity we can. The good news is we can always, always, always add Positivity, but sometimes it's just better math to reduce, eliminate, heal, or forgive the negativity.

It's the job of our managers to look for negative behaviors, to protect our team against them, and to do all that they can to transform those behaviors in the people they manage. Hopefully they don't allow negativity to breed due to their fear of confrontation, their negligence in paying attention, or their justification that we need those people's skills despite their bad attitude.

But it's our job, too, to reduce the negativity around us as much as we can. And by reduce, I don't mean simply ignoring it, swallowing it, gossiping to others about it, or stuffing it down. In all those cases, the negative feelings are still there. It's just more likely to keep rotting instead of healing. One of the most indelible studies I remember reading was one from Duke University Medical Center in which they coded the facial expressions of men who were coronary patients to identify how various emotions impacted their hearts. As expected, anger predicted myocardial ischemia—a medical term that basically means an abnormality or local deficiency of blood supply. But guess what other facial expression led to the same blood restriction? A "non-enjoyment smile."[13] Basically, that's the smile we do with our mouths but doesn't translate to the rest of our face. Fake smiles not only don't reduce the negativity, they add more to it!

We're much better off actually figuring out how to eliminate the frustration—which often means admitting it's there in the first place. Remember, there's always bound to be some negativity; the important thing is then how we respond to it, what we do to lessen it, and how we go about returning to a place of sincere positive emotion. We can do this by any number of things including setting boundaries, initiating awkward but important conversations, asking questions instead of assuming, creating better systems, communicating our expectations more clearly, committing to forgiving the person, or changing how we view the situation.

And in more cases that most of us would admit, we might be the one causing negativity for others. The common culprits: complaining, sulking, eye-rolling, staying quiet and not participating, talking too loudly, talking all the time, engaging in gossip, interrupting others, and judging others harshly. Look at yourself as a social scientist might, and ask yourself, "If I had to come up with one habit I do that could potentially annoy others, what might it be?" and explore what might help you minimize the harm.

POSITIVITY IS REQUIRED

I know, I know. It's not our fault. We're the smart, hardworking, talented, and fun ones! I'm going to give all of us reading this book the benefit of the doubt and agree that any negativity at work probably isn't *our* fault (where's the wink emoji when I need it?!?). But I do think maturity means taking responsibility wherever we can, even if we're not the obvious problem. We can remember:

1. Positivity is positive emotions.
2. Positivity is the result of our actions.
3. Positivity is the goal in every relationship.
4. Positivity must be higher than negativity.
5. Positivity doesn't mean no negativity, but we can reduce it.

It's crucial that we figure out how to experience more Positivity. Our workplaces will benefit, as will we personally, if we enjoy our work enough (Positivity) to want to keep showing up (Consistency) in an authentic way (Vulnerability). Without it feeling good, few of us will feel satisfied enough to want to practice the next requirement, Consistency.

THREE WAYS TO INCREASE POSITIVITY

1. **Start with Warmth.** Remember that those around us judge us by how they feel in our presence. At minimum: acknowledge people when you/they arrive, make eye contact, say their name, smile, and show some curiosity about their lives.
2. **Increase Our Appreciation.** Thank them when they do something for us, compliment them on things you notice, and congratulate them for accomplishments. Be known as someone who is generous with your recognition of others—especially when distracted, jealous, or drained.
3. **Respond with Empathy.** If they share good news, cheer with them; if they share frustration, groan a little with them; if they share excitement, express hope with them. Try not to let anyone express something that goes unvalidated. Even just a "thank you for sharing that with me" or a "I totally get it" will reduce the chances of them regretting their openness and will increase the chances for future connection.

THREE WAYS FOR MANAGERS TO INCREASE POSITIVITY

1. **Focus on Strengths.** Catch your team members doing what they do well and acknowledge their efforts. Start meetings off by asking all the team members to give an example of how they have used one of their strengths recently. Spend most of the employee reviews focused on how they can develop what they do best and where they feel most energized.

2. **Schedule Time That Promotes Amusement, Joy, Inspiration, Hope, or Awe.** Whether it's a few moments in every meeting, a fun break once a week at work, or a field trip away from the office—make a list (or better yet, have them help brainstorm a list) of what activities, events, and actions produce positive feelings on the team.
3. **Role-Play Empathy-Building Exercises.** Find opportunities for the team to practice "remembering" that others are just like us—whether they're our competitors, adversaries, or simply people we need to negotiate with, serve, or convince. I love how Paul Santagata, head of Industry at Google, leads his team through these reflections:

    - This person has beliefs, perspectives, and opinions, just like me.
    - This person has hopes, anxieties, and vulnerabilities, just like me.
    - This person has friends, family, and perhaps children who love them, just like me.
    - This person wants to feel respected, appreciated, and competent, just like me.
    - This person wishes for peace, joy, and happiness, just like me.[14]

How to Develop Relationships at Work That Are Consistent

Consistency, in short, is the time we spend interacting with each other to build trust. It's in interacting with each other that we develop a pattern, a norm, or a consistent way of being together that therefore increases our perception that we can predict how we each might respond in a certain situation. In other words, future trust is built on past Consistency.

And this one requirement, my dear friends, is single-handedly the main reason we bond with people at work even though they may not be the kind of friends we'd otherwise choose. Childhood, high school, and college are the top three ways we made our friends growing up; but move into adulthood, and our jobs top the list—because these are the places in our lives where we experience the most Consistency.

It's not that friendships happened automatically when we were kids as much as that Consistency happened automatically when we were kids. We had to go to school with the same kids every day—we didn't wait to be invited; we had to show up at our extracurricular activities, whether band practice, swimming meets, or soccer games—they were scheduled into our lives repeatedly; we had to have a roommate in college—proximity was never optional. And, now, for most of us, work is the most consistent thing we have in our lives. That Consistency is why we are most likely to bond with those we work alongside, whether we intend to or not.

Of course, there are people we spend consistent time with whom we don't end up liking, or trusting, because we lack Positivity and/or Vulnerability with them—so Consistency alone isn't enough. But as we start understanding the components of a healthy relationship, we'll quickly see that it's also impossible to ever enjoy others (Positivity) and get to know them (Vulnerability) without investing time (Consistency). This one matters big-time.

In our nonwork relationships, Consistency is the requirement that people complain is the hardest in the bulk of their friendships. Consistency takes the one thing that too many people feel is in scarce supply: time. It's one more thing to initiate, schedule, and organize.

But bring us to work, and the hardest requirement can often become one of the easiest—we're already there!

CONSISTENCY IS DEVELOPED

At the **bottom of the Triangle**, we don't yet feel secure commitment with someone based on a history of really being there for each other, but we can aim for reliable interactions. We don't need to trust them with our secrets, respect the way they do business, or enter into commitments with them. But our decision to create as reliable of interactions as possible will help us get our jobs done well.

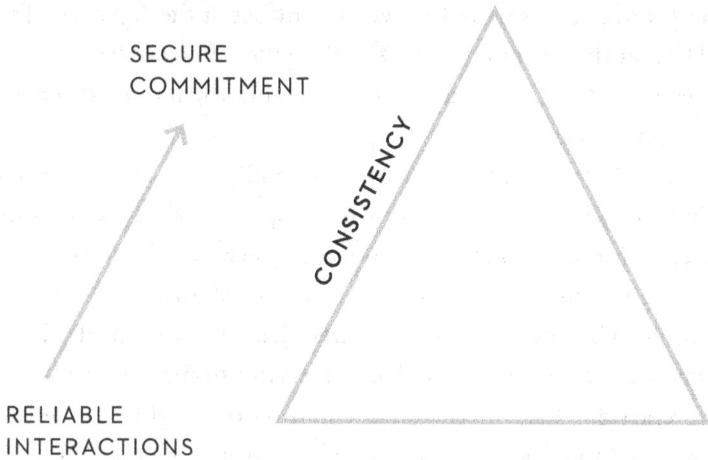

The goal of Consistency is to increase trust so that we feel safe with each other, which we do incrementally as we increase Positivity and Vulnerability. We need to feel as though we can rely on each other, which happens as we get to know each other and build history.

But just as friendship isn't all or nothing, neither is trust.

- We might not confide in a colleague because we don't know if we trust her not to use this personal information against us at some point, but that doesn't mean we don't trust her to do her job.
- We might not trust that a new customer will eventually join our loyalty program, but we can feel confident that he left our store or restaurant happy.
- We might not trust that our supervisor thinks we're ready for a promotion, but we can still feel that she appreciates our work in our current role.

The extent of what we can rely on in someone grows only as our experience with them increases.

Trust at the bottom of the Triangle is situational—at this meeting, during this shift, on this project, in this role—as opposed to the unlimited trust we might have for someone at the Top of the Triangle. Here, at the bottom, we don't confuse the difference between trusting people in this circumstance and expecting them to be that way in all circumstances.

In other words, we don't have to blindly trust everyone around us, but can we assume we'll both show up respectfully, stay focused on each other or our task, and accomplish what we're both trying to make happen? Can my coworkers count on me showing up when I said I would? Can my supervisor presume that I'll make the deadline? Can my sales manager expect that I'm trying to make a sale with every interaction? Can my customer count on the food being delivered as ordered? Can the workshop trainer safely assume that I'll pay attention and participate? Can the person whose business card I just collected at the networking event depend on me not sending a blizzard of sales emails? Basically, can I be trusted in this moment to be as competent and reliable as the occasion demands?

As we move up the Triangle, we practice being more reliable with each other by having consistent behaviors that lead to trust. We trust each other more in our collaborations and eventually extend that to other areas as we learn more about what we can come to expect from each other in various settings.

At the Top of the Triangle we experience *secure commitment,* where we both feel confident that the other person has our back, can be relied upon to support us, and holds themselves responsible for being present in our lives. Ideally, there is little need up there for insecurities, unanswered questions, or unspoken expectations because we feel meaningful transparency (highest level of Vulnerability) and complete acceptance (highest level of Positivity).

HOW TO DEVELOP CONSISTENCY

In our nonwork life we understand that if we want to spend time with someone we have to initiate it, because the chances are low that we'll simply "run into each other." But at work, for good and for bad, this is how most of our relationships start. It's good in that it allows us to build connections without having to extend invitations to near strangers to get together, schedule extra events into our full calendars, or start conversations without knowing a thing about the other. By both of us being in the same company, industry, or workplace, we already have conversation starters, opportunities to see each other, and a reason to connect. Where it can be bad, or limiting, is when we don't understand the role this Consistency has in our feeling close. Once we understand how we can increase it, or limit it, we can start to see how we can strengthen (or weaken) any relationship we want.

But time is an interesting thing. The answer to a healthier relationship isn't just *more* time. The reason time is important is because it's our interactions that build up the scaffolding of our relationship—the structure, the bones, the systems, the patterns, the expectations. Time is simply the product that builds our scaffolding and allows us to see the shape of that relationship—what we do together, where we do it, how we do it, and when we do it. What will we find we most enjoy talking about? Are we going to be friends who primarily text or email? Will we feel most supported with short and frequent interaction or wait for occasions where we can connect longer? What will be the activities we repeat the most often?

So, far more important than just increasing time is being more strategic and thoughtful about how we're using that time to build the interactions that matter most.

Consistency is the answer to the question "What is the norm for us?"

Consistency Starts with Proximity

Proximity, or the nearness in space we have to each other, is how most relationships start. If you broaden proximity to also include virtual proximity—those moments and reasons where our two worlds might come closer to each other via an email, phone call, or video conference—then it's safe to say that we will only form friendships with those in this world with whom we have reason to bump into, to meet, to interact with, because at some point proximity brought us together. But physical proximity is the biggest predictor of who we'll bond with.

Proximity does a number of things for us, including two worth mentioning here. The first benefit is that proximity increases our chances of liking each other! Simply seeing each other more often—what is called the mere-exposure effect—increases our familiarity and ups our odds of feeling closer, and safer.

Remember that police academy study I referenced in Chapter 3 when I was highlighting that the cadets didn't end up becoming friends based on common interests or personalities? On the contrary, much to the surprise of many, they ended up building close ties based on their name. More specifically, where their name fell on the roster, since all classes sat in alphabetical order. When graduating cadets listed the classmates with whom they had formed the closest relationship, 90 percent listed the individual they sat beside. They bonded based on proximity.

That study has been repeated a hundred times over in dorms, neighborhoods, schools, and workplaces around the world: we are more likely to be close to someone the closer we physically are to them. Despite the technology in our world that allows us to be friends with anyone on the planet—we still have the highest chances of feeling close to those we live with, or near, and those we work beside. In fact, we're six times more likely to form collaborative relationships with someone sitting near us, even if they work in a different department than we do, than we are to partner with someone from our own department if they work on a different floor.[1] Researchers can walk into nearly any workplace and predict with uncanny accuracy who we are probably close to simply by seeing whom we work beside. And it's mind-boggling, to say the least, to see the odds exponentially drop for every seat or office apart we are.

The second thing that proximity increases besides familiarity is the opportunity for spontaneous conversation. Proximity is why we we're more likely to strike up a conversation with the person beside us on the plane than the person behind us, why we might say hi to someone in an elevator whom we'd ignore if they were on the other side of the room, and why we feel closer to the colleagues whose offices or desks we have to walk by every day to get to ours.

Scientists, like Ben Waber, author of *People Analytics*, who have tracked our internal communication, have verified that no matter how we talk to each other—email, chat, face-to-face—the likelihood that we will communicate is directly proportional to the proximity of our desks. He says, "As you get pretty much onto different floors you might as well be in another city."[2] He has hundreds of examples of how much that proximity matters, including an interesting one in which engineers who worked next to each other were four times more likely to bring up a problem they were trying to solve in contrast to a team who worked remotely from each other.

The proximity we have to each other increases our creativity, problem-solving abilities, and overall performance. Daniel Coyle, best-selling author of *The Culture Code: The Secrets of Highly Effective Groups*, says, "Being in the same space together for vast chunks of time—physical, face-to-face proximity—that's the killer app. You're actually thirty-four times more likely to respond favorably to a request face to face versus email. If you're just talking about productivity, you can succeed alone, but if you're talking about creative groups, proximity ends up being really important."[3]

The power of proximity is what has led to so many workplaces being designed to maximize our human interaction: open-floor plans, cafés stocked with food, common spaces for recreation or socialization, commuter shuttle programs, and any other ways that encourage us to meet around the proverbial watercooler. It conversely begs us to be strategic about our workforce spread around the globe—whether, and how, we support remote working and how to best manage teams that don't share floor space. Continuing to learn just how powerful this proximity is will continue to inform our organizations as they think through which departments should share a floor, which teams should sit next to each other, and even which people are best next to each other.

And for each of us—whether we sit beside the same people every day, work in relative solitude from home, or are spending the bulk of every day interacting with different customers, it behooves us to ask: Is there anything I can do to intentionally be closer, even occasionally, to others so that we can increase our familiarity and allow for more spontaneous interaction that might enrich my work and life?

Consistency Accelerates with Intensity

Intensity, the strength or potency of an experience, is perhaps one of the rarer ways that time can bond us, but bond us quickly it can. We find typically that trust and reliability increase over time, but sometimes a shared experience can be so unique or powerful that it accelerates our trust in each other.

Some of us have jobs—such as in the armed forces or as first responders—where the term *foxhole buddy* literally means more than just someone with whom we've gone through something difficult or unique. A longitudinal study of veterans from World War II and the Korean War followed three groups of men—those who saw no combat, those who participated in combat but were never exposed to death, and those who participated in combat and were exposed to death. Besides the obvious correlations between the increase in danger leading to stronger camaraderie (notably they felt closer to someone with whom they shared battle conditions than someone they saw frequently in the mess hall), the bond lasted longer too. The researchers found that the veterans who were exposed to death together were nearly twice as likely to still be friends forty years later than those whose lives weren't at risk.[4]

But here's the kicker—while, certainly, intense experiences bond us more quickly than simply sitting next to each other—studies show that simply *believing* we are in something together has a similar effect. That's how powerful a frame can be—that simply perceiving to be *in* something together makes a huge difference. In a compelling study out of Stanford University, researchers found that when one group was treated like they were working together—even though they were each working alone in different rooms—they persisted 48–64 percent longer, reported more interest in the task, and performed better than those who simply worked by themselves, never believing that they were "together" in the exercise.[5]

Retreats, special projects, mergers, layoffs, crises, surprises, successes—anything that can produce intense feelings shared with others—has the potential to accelerate bonds as we are reminded that we're not "in it" alone.

Yoon became friends with Janet "for no other reason than we had to," she said with a bit of a smile. Basically, they were the only two female partners at a law firm. They actually did have a choice as they could have let fear whisper that they needed to compete with each other, but instead they took the shared experience of knowing what it felt like to be the only woman in the room and bonded over that unique commonality. Based on proximity alone, since they worked in different divisions, chances were low they would have become friends had they both been male, surrounded by plenty of other men with whom to connect. But the intensity of both being the minority in a group helped them feel like they were in a shared experience together as they used that commonality to accelerate their Consistency, Positivity, and Vulnerability.

If we want to feel like we belong at work, what are the ways we can reach out to others in the company with whom we might share a common feeling or experience? What are the activities we can initiate or lean into that might help us feel like we accomplished, or survived, together?

Consistency Increases with Frequency

Frequency, the regularity at which something is repeated, is usually made possible by proximity, but they aren't the same thing. We can put ourselves in someone else's proximity to increase the chance of connecting—say, at a networking event or conference—but frequency is when it's repeated. It's frequency that leads some of us to say some variation of "My coworkers know more about me than my dear friends!" By that we usually mean that we talk to our coworkers more frequently, so chances are they know more about what's going on in our day-to-day lives than many of our nonwork friends. If our frequency with a dear nonwork friend is only a monthly lunch or a weekly phone call, then we can quickly see how someone who sees us on Monday at work might hear more about our weekend than we'd think to tell our friend when we see them for lunch in two weeks.

The frequency we have at work is perhaps the largest motivation I felt for writing this book. Author Annie Dillard famously said, "How we spend our days is, of course, how we spend our lives." And there's no question for most of us that the largest portion of our days is spent at work. In fact, the average person among us will spend ninety thousand hours of our lives at work—a third of our lifetime. Dillard, less famously, then wrote, "What we do with this hour, and that one, is what we are doing."[6] Yes, we are working, but it's perhaps the biggest missed opportunity in the world if we aren't also using those hours to connect in satisfying ways.

Of course, frequency doesn't guarantee that what we share will be deep, meaningful, or personal, but it does set us up to experience a higher quantity of interactions with one another. And interactions we need! With over 140,000 Americans tracked with the Gallup-Healthways Well-Being Index, they have found a correlation between the number of social hours each day to our daily mood. The data suggests we need six hours of social interaction every day to lower our stress, minimize our anxiety, and leave us feeling connected. Compare the two-to-one ratio of happiness to stress if you get only one hour of social interaction in a day to the eleven-to-one ratio if you can hit the six-to-seven-hour mark![7] That sounds like a lot, and I doubt we all feel like we need that much, but in my *Friendships in the Workplace* survey, I asked respondents how they felt about the amount of interaction they get at work every day, and a whopping 36 percent said they wished for more! In contrast, only 11 percent wished for less.

How do you feel about the amount of interaction at work?				
Wish for Way Less	*Wish for Less*	*Good the Way It Is*	*Wish for More*	*Wish for Way More*
2%	9%	53%	32%	4%

And they aren't wanting more because they're not getting any. When they're asked how much of their daily job consists of interaction with their peers and with their clients, about two-thirds of us are already spending at least half of our time, or more, with others throughout the day.

	None	*Very Little*	*About Half*	*Quite a Bit*	*Almost All*
Peers/Team	3%	28%	27%	29%	13%
Clients/ Customers	9%	27%	23%	17%	24%

If I dig deeper in the data, we see that, unsurprisingly, the less we get, the more we want. For example, 60 percent of those who get no, or very little, time with their team members wish for more time with their team; but surprisingly, 20 percent of those who say they spend quite a bit or all of their time with their peers still want even more.

And, obviously, few of us just want more for the sake of more. Rather we want it with hopes that it leaves us feeling better. And it usually does. In line with other studies, we see once again that our time spent with colleagues is directly correlated with our energy. When I asked them, "How do you feel about the quality of interaction at work?" they were twice as likely to feel connected and energized if they spend almost all day with their team, as opposed to none at all.

	Disconnected/ Drained				*Connected/ Energized*
Very little time w/ peers/team	14%	21%	32%	22%	11%
Almost all time w/ peers/team	11%	4%	21%	41%	23%

Clearly, we all have different needs and preferences, but the important thing is paying attention to how much frequency we each feel like we need—and most of us need more.

One last correlation I found interesting is based on whether someone has a best friend at work. If so, they're 20 percent more likely than someone who doesn't have a best friend at work to be happy with the amount of interaction they have, half as likely to wish for more interaction, and five times more likely to report feeling very connected and energized.

That frequency obviously extends to our interactions with our boss or supervisor too. How frequent does the interaction need to be? Well, when more than 32,000 American and Canadian executives, managers, and employees were surveyed by IQ Leadership, they found that people who spent more time with their managers—up to a point—reported higher levels of inspiration, engagement, innovation, and intrinsic motivation. That point seems to be six hours a week.[8] Interestingly, their research also confirmed that to be true even for employees who didn't much like their boss. Apparently when we are getting that face-to-face time, we are more likely to recommend our company as a great place to work, we feel more inspired with our work, and we generate and share more ideas. Unfortunately, only about 4 percent of us are getting that important face-to-face interaction with our managers. While six hours might feel undoable for most managers and workplaces, hopefully we can at least let a study like this inspire us to ask, "How might I interact even a bit more frequently?"

Consistency Stabilizes with Repetition

Repetition, or the reoccurrence of an action or event, creates a structure or expectation of our time together that can leave us feeling safer, or closer, because we know what to expect. While frequency speaks to *how often* we might interact, repetition speaks more to *how similar* that interaction might look. Think of rituals, habits, practices, procedures, ceremonies, customs, and culture. Any time we are repeating what we say, how we say it, what we do together, how we do it, or even where we do it—we are tapping the power of repetition to bring people together and build bonds.

In other words, Consistency isn't just about spending *more* time together, but for that time to feel safe, we need it to feel reliable. It feels reliable when we've repeated it enough to be able to answer, "What can I expect?" The foundation of our culture is determined by all the things we repeat—or not.

- Can I walk into my office expecting to be greeted because that's how we do it?
- Do I walk into meetings feeling like I know what's coming because we have a pattern?
- Can I trust that if I send this email to my coworker that I'll hear back promptly because they've repeatedly proven that to be true?
- Do I know how this task helps my team because I've repeatedly heard the objectives?
- Do I feel safe suggesting a somewhat nontraditional idea because I've repeatedly seen others get praised for doing the same?
- Am I safe in assuming that if someone on my team has a problem with me that they'll come talk about it with me directly because we've role-played that and repeatedly said we'd prefer that over talking behind our backs?

It's repetition that moves the needle of trust, establishes expectations, and leads to effectiveness. A study of managers in the workplace whose communication was recorded and whose actions were shadowed showed that the "managers who were deliberately redundant moved their projects forward faster and more smoothly."[9] Indeed, redundancy outperformed power in getting things done quickly and more efficiently.

And the good news is that we don't have to just cross our fingers and hope that others step up to repetition—we can initiate it! We can ask our managers to clarify one more time what their goal is, and we can ask, "What can I do to increase the odds of hearing back from you more quickly?" We can be consistent, we can ask questions to inform our expectations, and we can kindly let people around us know what we're expecting.

Even with the more fun aspects of ritual-building, we have way more power than we often think. Certainly, we want our leaders and managers to think through what rituals could be created, supported, or implemented around things like new hires, team milestones, personal accomplishments, team events and meetings, birthdays and anniversaries, and failures and losses. But since few of us are in positions that might create the rituals for an entire brand or industry, what fascinates me is how powerfully even small and seemingly ordinary repetition can encourage more bonding and satisfaction in our workplaces.

Kara, an operations assistant for a skin-care brand, shared with me how much her coworkers loved her homemade green smoothies she shared one afternoon, so much so that she ended up deciding to make a different green smoothie for everyone each week on what is now affectionately called "Wellness Wednesday." Her boss wisely then started picking up the tab on the ingredients.

Salena, a senior project manager, said she and another manager unintentionally started a ritual walking one loop around the city block together after either of them has to do something tough—whether it's reprimanding an employee or looking at disappointing product-launch reports. Now either of them need only to pop into each other's office and say the word, "Walk?" and they know they'll have a few moments of fresh air and support.

Andy, on the other hand, was looking to have more fun with a few of his coworkers at his elementary school. Working in a primarily female-dominated workplace where they rarely saw each other without kids around, he said it felt challenging to feel connected to the other teachers. What started as him inviting a few other teachers to meet for drinks at a restaurant down the street one day after they had all turned in their quarterly report cards is now a quarterly ritual where all the teachers are invited. (And the PTA was only too happy to spread the word that gift certificates to said restaurant would be welcome teacher appreciation gifts!)

Allyson, an independent hair stylist who doesn't have colleagues, per se, since she "just rents a chair" next to other stylists, thought it would be fun to decorate the station of another stylist for her birthday. Of course, you can already guess that now they all gang up to make sure there's a little party in a chair for every stylist on her birthday.

In what ways might we start, and repeat, something that can bring us feeling closer to those around us?

Consistency Broadens with Variety

Variety, the diversity or lack of sameness, gives a relationship the well-rounded feeling that we have practiced different ways of being together. While it's not always the opposite of repetition, it does help provide a bit of yang to the yin of familiarity that every relationship eventually establishes. Spending time together doing something new, or unusual, together invites us to learn more about each other, strengthens our relationship as we add "one more thing" we do together in the story of our relationship, and often can be one of the ways we create meaningful memories.

Every relationship, while it needs its predictability and meaningful repetition, also thrives with some variety. Variety broadens the roads in our relationships by expanding our territory with each other, and it paves new roads that give us additional ways of interacting. Both outcomes strengthen our relationship and provide backup roads if one no longer works.

Variety is like cross-training a relationship, giving any two people, or group of people, more ways to know one another and have fun together. Variety—whether it's an escape room, scavenger hunt, ropes course, cooking class, or go-cart racing—is why the best team-building activities are the ones that don't feel like a typical day of work. Yes, we might roll our eyes a bit, but the truth is that opportunities to experience different sides of one another strengthen the side of us that works together. We build trust, increase our communication skills, and practice collaboration every time we step outside of our comfort zones together. The more we engage with one another in a variety of ways, the more that engagement spills over into our routine interactions and work.

But it's not just the creative off-site meetings, fun team-building exercises, and elaborate parties that our superiors may, or may not, plan that strengthen our team bonds. Any one of us can ask the question, "What can I do to get to know this annoying coworker, someone outside my department, my colleagues, or my new boss in another way?"

Morgan, a group fitness teacher, spent more time with her class attendees than with the other teachers. So when a couple of them started talking last year about an overnight trip to someone's cabin one weekend, she decided to join them. "I don't need them to be my friends," she assured me. "And, quite honestly, leading up to it, I would have preferred to just stay home and be with my family, but I could also see how spending a night together would give us something more to build on at work." So she committed. She jumped in and made new memories and got to know them outside of their work mode. And while she still doesn't view any of them as best friends, she not only enjoyed working with them more but said, "We now have a few inside jokes and, interestingly, I feel more supported at work. Like if one of us needs a favor in covering a class, we'd be more invested in helping each other."

And beyond seeking variety in our activities, I'd be remiss if I didn't also broaden the meaning of variety to include our communication—what we talk about, how we connect, and when we interact. If most of our interaction with a team member on the other side of the country is limited to email or phone—variety could be suggesting a video conference next time. If we see our client only when we're collaborating on a big deal, variety could be surprising him with a phone call with some good news in between deals. If we only talk about what's not working on our computer every time the IT person is in our office, variety could be asking her how she initially got into being everyone's go-to fixer. Anything that helps broaden the relationship, giving us one more conversation, memory, or method of communication is variety that bonds.

Consistency Lasts with Duration

Duration, the length of time we've known each other, is one of the strongest correlations to how much we will, or will not, trust each other. The longer we've experienced someone being a certain way, the more likely we are to feel like we know them. The more history we share, the safer we feel predicting our future interactions.

While workplaces, and how we spend time interacting within them, vary widely, what we do know is that every relationship is developed over time—and the longer the time spent, the closer we're likely to feel. In fact, Dr. Jeffrey Hall, from the University of Kansas, has been researching this very aspect of bonding by asking, "How long does it take most of us to start feeling close to someone?" People's answers, while conducted outside of a work setting, remind us that relationships are indeed developed over time. People report needing about fifty hours with someone to move from stranger to casual friend, about eighty to a hundred hours to feel like friends, and about two hundred hours before we feel the closeness of being best friends.[10]

Obviously, it looks different at work where we may not be spending quality hours getting to know each other. But every relationship is an investment of time, and the more time we've shared, the more we'll feel like we know each other.

REMOTE WORKING, GLOBAL TEAMS, AND WORKING ALONE

How to Feel Close When Consistency Doesn't Include Proximity

When we realize the important role Consistency has in our relationships, we also then realize why loneliness shows up as one of the biggest downsides to working alone. Considering all of us who work off-site, work for ourselves, are part of global teams, participate in the growing "gig economy," or telecommute part of the time, that's almost 50 percent of us who need to become more skilled in relationship-building strategies when face-to-face interaction with the same people isn't the norm.[11]

The answer to our workplace loneliness is to look to add other ways, besides proximity, to build Consistency with our colleagues. The good news is that in my *Healthy Team Relationship Assessment*, the teams who work remotely frequently score as high, or higher, than teams who work together because they've been forced to be more strategic to foster their Consistency and not take it for granted. Here are some of their tips:

1. **Schedule the Consistency.** Without fail, the teams who are doing it well are doing so because they have scheduled the frequent and regular interaction that leaves them feeling closer to each other. They aren't leaving it to chance or connecting only when there's an urgent need or focused agenda.

One team has a group video chat every Monday where they each talk about their upcoming objectives that week and then, again, every Friday where they all debrief. Another team works virtually every morning together for two hours through video, online chatting, and collaboration software to maximize their interaction before spending the rest of their day doing their own tasks. Another team pops on video for thirty minutes every morning to each share one thing they want to tell everyone about, and one thing for which they would like more support. Managers, especially, have found it critical to schedule more regular one-on-ones with their remote workers to ensure they have clear and measurable outcomes, are receiving helpful feedback and validation, and ensure they feel they have easy access to their company and its mission.

But we don't need to fall victim to bad leadership if that Consistency isn't as much as we'd like. We can reach out to our manager to suggest more clear ideas for increased connection by asking, "Would you be willing to schedule a more regular one-on-one with me to make sure I stay connected to your vision and can support you the best way possible?" Or, "Would you be willing to experiment with scheduling a weekly video call with our whole team for the purpose of simply brainstorming and collaborating on various projects, in addition to the staff meeting we have where we're more updating each other?" Or, "Would you mind if I started a channel in our collaboration software that is simply designed for us to each 'share one thing every day that others might need to know' to help make sure that those in the office are also updating those of us who are working remotely?"

And we can most certainly schedule our own Consistency by reaching out to various team members, being reliable with responding promptly, letting our team know when we're working and/or will be available, and by participating as fully as possible in any and all gatherings and team meetings.

2. Prioritize video and in-person communication as much as possible. While it takes more energy to look presentable, we also feel closer when we can see one another's faces. Neuroscience has shown us that empathy is developed when our mirror neurons are able to mimic the micro expressions of other people, so we're more likely to feel invested in, and empathetic toward, those whose feelings we can intuitively see. As a team, be clear which modes of communication are preferred in which scenarios, and give preference to in-person, or video, as we're able.

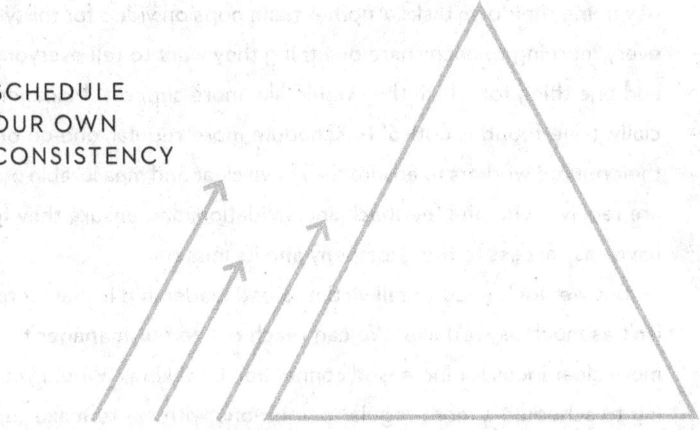

For some, this means prioritizing coming into the office occasionally (one study showed that telecommuting up to two and a half days a week had no negative effects on the relationships[12]), even when we're not required, to simply communicate that they matter and that we value feeling connected. This could mean, when traveling near one of our colleagues—either for business or personal reasons—that we reach out and see if we can schedule a lunch while we're in their vicinity. This could also be as easy as asking, "Hey, do you mind if we switch this over to video? I'd love to see you!" And, above all, it means when we are together in any way with our colleagues, we will do all we can to maximize that time by staying off our phones, participating fully in team-building activities, and showing interest in everyone.

3. **And remember that Consistency is simply the foundation for the other two requirements of friendship: Vulnerability and Positivity.** A team that simply stays in touch and communicates well may be efficient, but it doesn't prevent loneliness or increase our commitment and loyalty to that team or job. So beyond simply having consistent interaction, we also need to aim to have some of the interaction focused purely on relationship building.

Good managers will make sure that there are video calls for the purpose of celebrating, getting to know a new employee, and asking everyone what more is needed from one another to feel better connected. They will make use of the technology that ensures that every employee is having a thirty-minute phone call each week with someone different on the team just for the purpose of getting to know each other, that new employees feel there is an accelerated pathway for getting to know their team, and that there's time for each employee to feel seen by the team outside of projects. They will create online conversations that help the team get to know one another, inspire one another, and laugh together. They will schedule virtual happy hours or team lunches designed to help their team hang out with one another. And when they bring everyone together, they will maximize making memories, laughing, and connecting.

But we can do that too. Now that we understand that without us sharing parts of ourselves with each other (Vulnerability) or taking the time to enjoy one another (Positivity) that it's *us* who suffer the most, we'll be proactive to not just view our jobs as a means to an end but as a gateway to meaningful connection. We'll put it on ourselves to contribute to the glue that will help our team feel close. We'll text appreciation to our colleagues, we'll initiate lighthearted moments in virtual hangouts, we'll invite a colleague to virtual lunch, and we'll be sure to help others feel closer to us by offering up glimpses of who we are and what we love. We'll brainstorm a "safe word" for everyone on our team so that all we have to do is message that word when we're feeling isolated or lonely and we'll make sure someone jumps on a quick fifteen-minute call to just say hi!

The most important thing we can do, wherever we work, is see how important it is for our sakes to foster the connection that will keep us engaged. We can't enjoy one another or feel known if we don't have a regular way of connecting—so we'll set up what we need. Additionally, we'll take responsibility, on our end, beyond the relationships with our team and manager, to decide how much we need to work at a coworking space or café, attend association meetings regularly, and schedule more lunches or events with clients and friends to offset the interaction we're missing from working alongside a team.

We can absolutely have the flexibility we desire and the relationships we need if we're willing to value connecting the way we value productivity.

CONSISTENCY IS REQUIRED

The more ways we practice proximity, intensity, frequency, repetition, variety, and duration, the more glue we have bonding us, the more scaffolding we have protecting our relationship, the more threads are intertwined to make our rope stronger. The healthiest relationships are the ones who practice as many of the different paths of Consistency as possible.

1. Consistency starts with proximity.
2. Consistency accelerates with intensity.
3. Consistency increases with frequency.
4. Consistency stabilizes with repetition.
5. Consistency broadens with variety.
6. Consistency lasts with duration.

We can't practice every path of Consistency with every person, but we now know what it takes to be a reliable person, to form bonds with others, and to have clearer expectations on what exactly we are trusting someone to do, or not. We need far more positive Consistency at work to leave us all feeling as supported, safe, and happy as possible.

But all the Positivity and Consistency in the world can only take us so far without the third requirement: Vulnerability.

THREE WAYS TO INCREASE CONSISTENCY

1. **Be Proactive about Proximity.** Purposely sit in different spots in meetings to ensure you're bonding with different people. Volunteer on projects and teams with people whom you'd like to know better. Attend social events. Basically, keep putting yourself where people are in small groups and you will get to know one another.

2. **Say Yes to Variety.** Instead of begrudgingly participating in off-site meetings, new activities, or social functions—recognize them as the bonding activity that they can be and add your energy to the mix. Or initiate it. Invite the team over for a barbecue, offer up your living room to watch a season finale everyone's been talking about, or invite someone out to lunch.
3. **Value Reliable over Ideal.** Others will trust us based on what we do deliver, not on what we intended to deliver. It's better to respond with a quick email than to wait for time to write the perfect email . . . only to then forget. It's better to ask clarification questions now than to try to wow them by reading their minds and failing. It's better to consistently be on time than try to make up for it with lots of jokes. It's better to give a coworker five minutes of our attention now than to keep waiting for "when we both have time." Trust is built on tiny little consistent actions that build up over time.

THREE WAYS FOR MANAGERS TO INCREASE CONSISTENCY

1. **Encourage Connecting.** Smile when you see team members talking and socializing, backing it up with "Love that you two are connecting!" to minimize the risk of them feeling guilty. Talk frequently at staff meetings about resources within the organization (mentorship programs, employee resource groups, social events, mental health programs) so that your team knows what's available and knows you support it. Basically, keep giving permission to them to value their social experience.
2. **Establish Consistent Rhythms.** Set regular team meetings and one-to-one sit-downs so that your team knows not only when to expect time with you but also what they can expect during that time. That might mean agendas sent out early for those who

need time to process ahead of time, meetings they can trust won't be moved, and flow that feels familiar.

3. **Ask Each Person What Support Looks Like to Them.** Regularly ask some version of "What do you need from me to feel supported in this task or on this team?" Or "What would help you feel more ________ (safe, connected, trusting)?" Maybe followed up by "What might that look like?" And commit to either delivering what they need or taking responsibility to negotiate with them until landing on something that is deliverable and meaningful.

7

How to Develop Relationships at Work That Are Vulnerable

Of the Three Requirements, Vulnerability is undoubtedly the scariest one for most of us—especially in the workplace. When we think about encouraging it in the workplace, our brains conjure up images of employees crying in boardrooms, of employees gossiping and processing their personal drama instead of working, and of awkward trainings where we might all have to share our feelings.

But ask us what we want most from our coworkers and we'll say things like:

- "I just want to feel appreciated for what I am doing."
- "I want to feel safe sharing my ideas without feeling judged."
- "It'd be nice to know my boss actually cared about me, as a person, not just as a means to an end."

- "I wish I didn't feel like I had to conform in order to be valued."
- "I can see what we need, but no one ever asks me for my opinion."

Then, ask the leaders and they'll add to the list:

- "I wish I knew what my team really thought. Sometimes I'm afraid they just tell me what they think I want to hear."
- "I think my team is capable of more, but that they're so afraid of failure they prefer to play it safe."
- "I often feel caught in the middle—feeling like I have to toe the party line and yet wanting to just be honest with them about what's going on."
- "I struggle between wanting to be closer to my team and worrying that then they won't respect me."
- "Sometimes I wish I was allowed to simply say, 'I don't know the right answer,' without feeling like I'd look weak or incompetent."

And you'll see that despite our fears of Vulnerability gone bad, it's actually Vulnerability at work that we desperately want. Not because we're eager to come in and disclose our personal lives, but because we know how important it is to feel *seen* for who we are, even at work—or, maybe, especially at work. To that point, what continuously correlates with higher level of loneliness at work is how people answer the question about whether they "have to hide their true selves at work."[1] We want to be accepted for who we are. Work is not only where we spend most of our lives, but it's where we're making one of our biggest contributions. Why would we not want that significant side of us seen, recognized, valued, and accepted?

VULNERABILITY IS DEVELOPED

At the bottom of the Triangle, it's not appropriate to confide and process our lives with someone with whom we don't have a history of Consistency, but we can aim to be genuine in sharing who we are and be curious in learning more about the other. We won't tell others everything about what we're thinking, reveal our lives to them, or probe for juicy details—but we can aim to show up with authenticity in the context in which we're connecting. At a bare minimum, we will show up with *genuine interest*—for who they are, in what we're willing to share about ourselves, and for what this relationship could become.

The goal of Vulnerability is to get to know each other, which we do incrementally as we practice Consistency and Positivity with someone. When we're asked what matters most to us in a relationship, most of us rank honesty at, or very near, the top.[2] We want to believe that people are showing us who they *really* are, and we deeply want to believe we can do the same, without fear of judgment, exclusion, or punishment.

But, Vulnerability, perhaps more than Consistency or Positivity, is the one requirement our culture struggles with the most when it comes to "how much?" How honest should we be? How expressed can we be? How much of "us" can we show? How many of the details can we whisper? The Triangle provides us with the visual reminder that, again, it's not *whether* to be honest, but to what degree.

Our goal is to be authentic in a way that is balanced by the level of relationship we have with someone. As we move up the Triangle, we will both practice increasing our Vulnerability in our shared context, eventually moving to sharing more in other areas of our lives, and slowly moving up to levels where we're not only each sharing, but where we're more likely to be processing our feelings, confiding our fears and shame, and shining proudly in who we are.

At the Top of the Triangle we experience *meaningful transparency,* both feeling that we either know everything there is to know about the other person, or at least that we're willing to explore it together. Ideally, there is little need up there for filters, masks, or off-limit

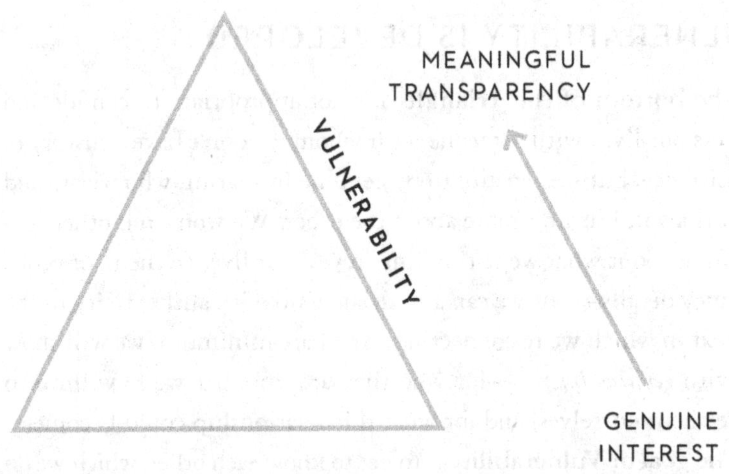

subjects because we feel secure in our commitment (highest level of Consistency) and complete acceptance (highest level of Positivity).

The most important thing is to keep in mind that there is a spectrum, a range of what's appropriate to share and who needs to know what. We must work to find a baseline on which we can try to show up with as much genuine interest as any specific context calls for when interacting with most people. Then, with those who matter to us, we can hopefully move those relationships up the Triangle as we increase Vulnerability in conjunction with Consistency and Positivity.

HOW TO DEVELOP VULNERABILITY

Vulnerability, the willingness to lower our defenses and drop our protective armor, is the only way we will ever be seen. We might feel safe if we keep that smile plastered on our face, that polished image on our social media profiles, that commanding personality that makes people fear us, that poker face that leaves us feeling like we have the upper hand, or that ability to hide our feelings behind our jokes and laughter; but that pretense of safety comes at a huge cost of not really feeling known, seen, or understood.

If we want a high-performing team—either because we want to enjoy our time at work more or because we care about accomplishing our goals—then it's not a matter of *if* we need more Vulnerability, but rather *how* we can create that "psychological safety" that is present in the best of teams.

In some ways, this might be the hardest chapter in the book to write, because "appropriate Vulnerability" will undoubtedly look very different in each of our contexts. A group of social work case managers might routinely end the day debriefing their cases with one another, talking about when they were personally triggered, and safely expressing their feelings. But it's less expected that a group of lawyers would make the time to do the same, what with the valuing of billable hours, their likelihood of being out with clients, and being in an industry in which facts trump feelings. And while we can attest that lawyers represent one of the loneliest professions (so something probably needs to change), it's beyond the scope of these pages to be able to determine what the ideal looks like for every industry, team, or culture.

But there are four guidelines I'd like to suggest, the first one filled with a long list of ways we *could* potentially practice Vulnerability no matter where we work.

Vulnerability Is More Than Disclosure

Vulnerability is not about everyone telling everyone everything. Not even close.

On the contrary, what we're going for isn't necessarily more disclosure as much as it's more authenticity, empathy, curiosity, and courage. This isn't about bringing more of our personal life drama to work as much as it's about having the bravery to deal with the drama that *is* work. This isn't about asking everyone on our team to reveal more as much as it's about reducing judgment interruptions, and the fear of being embarrassed if we think outside the box. Vulnerability isn't always about saying more as much as it's about showing up more—showing up with honesty and hope when morale is down, showing up with courage and resilience when change is inevitable, showing up with kindness and clarity when hard conversations beckon.

Vulnerability is the remembering that we are human beings whose hearts and feelings not only can't be shut off for eight hours a day but that we wouldn't want them to be. We know that we aren't our greatest despite our feelings, but because of them. Our Vulnerability is what allows us to celebrate our team wins, innovate creative solutions, empathize with our customers, and forgive our leaders for not living up to our expectations.

Vulnerability is the portal to feeling accepted, good enough, wanted, and valued. We want our vast experience to be helpful, our strengths to be appreciated, our ideas to be taken seriously, and our contributions to matter. For that to happen, we have to be willing to let those experiences, strengths, ideas, and contributions be seen. To feel accepted, we have to feel known; and to feel known, we have to reveal ourselves.

Examples of Vulnerability at Work

Brainstorming and Problem Solving. For many, this is one of the most vulnerable actions we can take—the sharing of our ideas. What if no one thinks it's a good idea? Or worse, what if everyone goes in this direction, it doesn't work, and I feel responsible?

In consulting various companies, I find myself in conversations all too frequently with employees who say something along the lines of, "It's so frustrating because all he would have to do is . . ." Then a cascade of wisdom about what they wish their supervisor would do comes pouring out. To which I always ask, "Have you shared this with them?" Nine out of ten people say no. Oh, some will assure me that their boss wouldn't listen or try to convince me it doesn't really matter—they can just keep doing their job. But their venting behind the supervisors' backs not only hurts the team that might benefit from that idea, but these employees are clearly frustrated and ultimately less engaged as they convince themselves that their ideas don't matter.

One of the most powerful acts of brave Vulnerability we can practice is voicing our opinions and ideas. That doesn't mean pushing them, fighting for them, or refusing to support other ways, but it does mean being willing to speak up when we see a problem and offer solutions when we can.

One manager of an internal communications team I worked with bravely, and vulnerably, led one team off-site meeting by asking all the people on her team to anonymously write down one problem they saw that they thought was either hurting the team or was a missed opportunity. She then wrote them all up on the whiteboard and facilitated a conversation about how these problems might be addressed.

As we build our relationships with one another, we practice "psychological safety," which is the one most necessary ingredient on every high-performing team. We have to believe that we can say something without being embarrassed, dismissed, ostracized, or punished.

Celebrating, Cheering, and Pride. Vulnerability isn't only acknowledging the shame we feel around our insecurities, but it's also recognizing we have just as much, if not more, shame around our success.

Pride, like joy, is one of the feelings that brings the most Positivity, and yet it's a vulnerable feeling that comes with guilt for far too many. Pride doesn't mean we think we're better than everyone, just as to feel inspired doesn't mean we think we're more inspired than everyone. We can feel pride, and should feel pride, and still celebrate and cheer for the success of others. True humility isn't thinking less of ourselves, downplaying our success, or dismissing compliments; true humility sees how amazing we are and believes that everyone else is too. We don't need more false humility in this world, and we definitely don't need more people thinking less of themselves. We have big problems, and we need people who believe they can solve them. If Vulnerability is about being seen, then of course, we definitely want to be seen for our good too.

I routinely ask my friends, "Tell me something you're proud of in your life right now." I figure if we can't practice being proud with our friends, then what chance do we have of showing up in the world with the confidence we need for facing the critics, the obstacles, and the fears? The workplace, in embracing more Vulnerability, has the chance to also shine brighter.

Showing Our Creativity. Sharing our creativity, in any form, is one of the most vulnerable acts because not only does creativity hinge so very much on uncertainty, but it can so often feel like a piece of us is on display, naked.

While some industries live in the world of creativity—advertising, performance art, music, fashion, research and development, media, and architecture, to name a few—creativity is a skill that is in growing demand across our workforce. A recent IBM study of 1,500 CEOs revealed that creativity is the single most important skill for leaders,[3] and in a workforce preparedness study conducted by The Conference Board, 97 percent of employers said that creativity is of increasing importance.[4]

But we won't have it on our team without practicing Vulnerability. Our employees aren't going to volunteer that risk in a vacuum.

This was brought home for me as I recently facilitated an off-site meeting for a design team that scored high in Vulnerability. At first, I had been surprised because they all work remotely, which often isn't correlated to high Vulnerability scores. And they had such diversity on the team that commonalities that might have helped them feel close weren't immediately apparent. But, as Lee said, "Hey, when every week you're each putting your ideas and designs in front of each other, knowing the end product will look nothing like what you are starting with, you have no choice but to be vulnerable."

A couple things we can learn from teams that practice this skill regularly: the more you do it, the easier it becomes as you get less attached to any one form of your creativity; and the more everyone does it, the more likely everyone learns to practice empathy, Positivity, and encouragement as they all know what it feels like to have their work on display.

Responding to Conflict. It is not conflict that hurts a relationship, or organization, as much as our response to that conflict. The two most damaging responses tend to be avoiding the frustration and letting it fester in order to keep a façade of peace, or blowing up bombs of blame, shame, and anger.

The cost of ignoring conflict, in addition to the missed opportunity to learn more about each other and build the trust that we can solve problems together, is high turnover, passive-aggressive communication, a dysfunctional team, loss of productivity, and broken trust.

And I'll guess that most conflicts we avoid aren't some clear and obvious malicious monsters everyone on the team sees. Yes, there is bullying, blatant grievances, and palpable problems, but it's frequently the less straightforward conflicts that we dodge: giving honest feedback to an employee, sharing our disagreement on the best approach to a problem, telling a coworker we took offense to his or her comment, or not expressing a need we have for our workplace comfort and effectiveness.

Jacob says that while he has a lot of good ideas, he hates "fighting about the best way forward, so it's easier to just sit back and let everyone else figure it out." To have people back down, wait and see, or simply withdraw is not only a massive loss of possibility for the organization and team, but it means one more employee who doesn't feel *seen*. Ironically, it's often the people who hate conflict the most who have the greatest superpower for bringing harmony to a team, if only they'd be willing to stay engaged and help influence the tone of the conversation.

Learning how to confront issues in mature and healthy ways takes incredible Vulnerability. We know what to expect if we just swallow our feelings (or go home and complain to someone else when we're in charge of the narrative!), but we step right into uncertainty when we choose to engage. Vulnerability invites us to be less defensive, more present, and in touch with our feelings—all qualities that can turn conflict into connection.

Honoring Diversity and Inclusion. Diversity isn't just getting our numbers right, it's making sure we hear more voices, experiences, and perspectives. In other words, diversity for optics isn't the same as diversity when we really *see* the unique contribution. But that takes Vulnerability, because we don't know what we don't know.

All too often we hire diversity because we love the idea of having new voices added into the mix, and yet in reality we don't bring the curiosity that encourages those voices. To hire them means we may have to learn to do things differently. To welcome them means admitting our viewpoint isn't the only, or the best, one. To hear them means we have to stop speaking and start listening. Those calls are all born from Vulnerability—that place where we don't have complete control.

If our goal is for our employees "to feel seen in a safe and satisfying way," then how can we ask questions in a way that assures them we not only won't punish them for their answers but will appreciate their perspective? Are we willing to hear the answers to "What might we not see that you do?" or "What might you need that we haven't thought of yet?" To ask this of our oldest and youngest employees; to ask this of people with different work styles, strengths, and personalities; to ask this of those who come from other countries, religious backgrounds, and political leanings; to ask this of the minority gender, ethnicity, and sexual orientation; to ask this of those who have physical or mental challenges; to ask this of those who have worked primarily outside of our industry—this is what it means to value diversity.

Living with chronic pain, Peter expended so much energy every day simply trying to hide this truth. He downplayed it, minimized it, and tried to pretend it simply didn't bother him. But when a friend asked him, "If you could change anything at work, what would it be?" it got him thinking how even a few hours of working alone in quietness every afternoon would feel like a game changer. His friend then responded, "That's not an impossible request, you know." An eventual conversation with his boss inspired her to ask everyone on the team that same question, which resulted in a lot of people feeling like their needs were taken seriously.

Jaysmine, an African American woman, says she just wishes that people weren't so afraid of talking about racism at her workplace. "I can't tell you how many times I've watched us avoid the conversations we need to have because our senior leaders are afraid of saying or doing the wrong thing." It takes Vulnerability to say, "We won't do this perfectly, but we want to try. Will you help us?"

Our companies won't benefit from the beauty of diversity until, and unless, we are vulnerable enough to let those diversified voices impact and change us.

Apologizing. Apologizing is a tricky business. It's perhaps one of the most courageous choices a human can make, because it's truly a lowering of our defenses. "We are wired for defensiveness," says psychologist Harriet Lerner, author of *Why Won't You Apologize?* "It's very hard for humans to take clear and direct responsibility for specifically what we have said or done."[5]

We don't always know how the other person will respond. Will it lead to the outcome we hope for? What will they end up thinking about us? How will we feel afterward? Furthermore, most of us don't even know how to do it well, when we should do it, or why. But apologies—recognition that we broke a social rule, unintentionally or not—can do more to repair trust in a relationship than nearly any other act of Vulnerability. An apology tells the other person we *see* them and their hurt feelings and that we care enough to want to reestablish better expectations.

But here's the tricky part: the answer isn't for all of us to apologize more.

Much has been said about women's tendency to over-say "sorry." We apologize for asking someone to fix what they messed up, for having a differing opinion, for taking someone's time, and for expecting people to do their job. Vulnerability in many situations might mean being brave enough to take up space without apologizing.

Conversely, considering that our culture has not been stellar at encouraging, modeling, or expecting men to practice Vulnerability, it would make sense that those muscles probably aren't as well developed. Lerner points out that while "in all cultures studied, men apologize less frequently than women," it's not because they refuse to do it as much as that they don't think they've done *anything* wrong.

Gabriel lamented to me, "I honestly didn't think I needed to apologize. I obviously didn't mean to offend her and she tends to be overly sensitive." But he said that watching the news of men in power refusing to apologize to people whom they've hurt softened him enough to try. The connection left him feeling greater respect for her and increased trust in their working relationship.

Whether we each fit those gender norms or not, the gift in Vulnerability is for each of us to be more reflective as we ask ourselves if we are more likely to hide behind our apologies or our defensiveness. But either way, our goal is to hide less.

And the list could go on. It takes Vulnerability to:

- Ask for help, support, or resources.
- Admit we don't know the answer.
- Risk and reward failure.
- Share how we feel about a situation, conversation, or idea.
- Reveal our personal crises and disabilities when we need extra support.
- Be touched or impacted by the stories of injustice in our line of work.
- Tell someone about the inappropriate behavior we experienced or witnessed.
- Stand up for ourselves and ask for what we need.
- Resist conformity and value uniqueness.
- Try a new method, to experiment.
- Give and receive feedback without defensiveness and blame.

Hopefully, we can all nod our heads in agreement that our workplaces would be better off if we had more healthy examples of Vulnerability.

Vulnerability Inherently Comes with Risk So Don't Wait for It to Feel Easy

We've got to realize that risk isn't something to avoid, no more than we should try to avoid sweating when we exercise. When we want to push ourselves physically, we understand that sometimes that means gulping for air in a sprint, grunting through one more rep with heavier weights, or stretching a little further in our yoga move. We aren't shocked when there's discomfort, or even a little soreness. And the same is true for innovation, leadership, and personal growth: there's no way to achieve it without awkwardness, a little emotional sweat, and risk.

Feeling uncomfortable isn't a sign that it's wrong, bad, or to be avoided; on the contrary, when we're changing culture, learning new skills, and getting to know people in more meaningful ways, discomfort is to be expected. Even those of us reporting insecurity in our conversational skills, social anxiety, and shyness can't allow those to prevent us from participating. We can pay attention to our energy to help inform us how we might need to engage differently, or more thoughtfully, but we can't let it stop us. Even the most extreme introverts still need to be seen and feel connected.

Now the obvious caveat is that there's a big difference between discomfort and an injury. The goal, as you'll see in the next principle, is to train up to Vulnerability in such a way that we keep everyone as safe as possible. But to be clear: we won't reach healthy Vulnerability without some anxiety, resistance, or heavy breathing along the way. What that means is that we don't judge whether to practice it based on whether we feel fear or not. We will. Almost always.

Every time we choose to show up with authenticity, find the courage to voice our opinion, decide that we're going to ask for what we need, or risk not conforming to groupthink or traditional culture, we will risk something. Sometimes it's risking being misunderstood or judged; sometimes it may mean risking our paycheck, our reputation, or our brand.

We practice it because we value what's on the other side: We value courage and innovation. We value diversity and inclusion. We value impossible solutions to our massive problems. We value love, acceptance, and hope. We value personal and emotional health. We value bold ideas, brave leadership, and high ethics. We value human connection and healthy relationships. We value feeling seen and seeing others. None, absolutely none, of these things are possible without Vulnerability.

To that point, I love the story that Dr. Brené Brown, the leading expert on Vulnerability, shares in *Dare to Lead* about asking one question to several hundred military special forces. Instead of spending her time trying to convince them that Vulnerability wasn't a sign of weakness, she simply asked, "Can you give me a single example of courage that you've witnessed in another soldier or experienced in your own life that did not require experiencing Vulnerability?" And, of course, no one could.[6]

Vulnerability Must Be Practiced Safely

Similar to how we'd never advocate running a marathon without building up to it, Vulnerability is best practiced in incremental and escalating ways. In general, our Vulnerability should match, or be balanced, with our Consistency. The lower we are on the Triangle with each other—due to not knowing each other well, or because that relationship doesn't feel safe due to lack of consistent behavior—then our Vulnerability will appropriately be low to reflect that. Just because we know Vulnerability is the way to connection doesn't mean we want to be, or should be, connected closely to everyone.

As we increase our Consistency, feeling as though we have a structure, or pattern, for our relationship that feels reliable, we can practice increased Vulnerability. As we develop a history with each other of not being punished for sharing, we will feel more safe stretching what we can reveal or share.

In that study dubbed "The 36 Questions to Fall in Love" in which researchers validated that bonding had less to do with matching people up and more to do with helping them get to know each other, they found that the methodology with the highest success rate for consistently bonding people was "sustained, escalating, reciprocal, personalistic self-disclosure." The best way to help build a relationship is to continue to share bits and pieces of ourselves with each other in an incremental and ongoing way.[7] Not all at once, but bit by bit, we create a strong bond.

The Best Vulnerability Starts with, and Leads Back to, Positivity

But we don't want just any bond. We want a positive bond that feels good to both people, and to the whole team. That's why we mustn't forget that while the two arms up the sides of the Triangle—Consistency and Vulnerability—must increase incrementally, they both rest on the base of Positivity.

Which, as a reminder, ideally comes before, during, and after anything we share with each other. In other words:

- We initially need something to feel good enough that we want to share something.
- Then, while we're sharing, we're looking for minor acts of Positivity to encourage us to keep sharing—whether that's a nodding head, eye contact, sustained interest, appropriate reactions, or follow-up questions.
- And, after we share, when we're at risk of feeling our most exposed—after the joke, the whispered insecurity, the exposed emotion, or the potentially silly idea—what we need more than anything is validation that we made the right decision to share.

It sounds so easy to validate someone for sharing, but I've encountered many Vulnerability hangovers that could have been prevented had a particular response been offered.

One of the most powerful ways we can transform culture is to become swifter with our positive responses. Every time we can thank people for what they shared, express affirmation for what they tried, or validate the feeling they expressed—we decrease the odds of them walking away feeling unseen or misunderstood, and we increase the odds of them feeling safer next time.

And when it's our turn to practice Vulnerability, one of the best ways we can help others give us the Positivity we need is to encourage the response we most want. By saying, "Hey, I want to share what might be a harebrained idea with you, but instead of judging it, I'm hoping you could help me think through how we might theoretically make it happen," we increase the odds of the support we want. We can respond to someone's unsolicited advice with, "Thank you so much for trying to solve this, but honestly, what I think would feel better to me is simply your sympathy right now," to hopefully spark his compassion instead of his fixing. We can get back on the sharing train after someone interrupts us or sidelines the conversation with, "Sorry, I wasn't quite done sharing yet . . . hopefully you'll give me a few more minutes of attention," to invite her to better listening. We don't have to walk away feeling unseen just because others aren't reading our minds.

Granted, I know all of this can sound hard to do, if not impossible. But asking for what we need is at the heart of Vulnerability. To share something is one thing, but to admit it matters to us, and that the response of someone else can impact us, is perhaps one of the most vulnerable places to be. And yet, it's through this portal that closeness and safety are developed.

Remind yourself of these two truths as often as you can:

1. Most people didn't wake up today wanting to disappoint us or respond in any way that hurts us.

2. And most people haven't been trained in relationship health, so they don't know what they don't know.

Both truths remind us that we don't need to take their responses personally, and if anything, we just need to keep showing up with a willingness to model the contagious behaviors we hope to someday see from them.

VULNERABILITY IS REQUIRED

Our workplaces will benefit, as will we personally, if we believe we're seen in a way that feels safe and satisfying. We can do that when we practice healthy Vulnerability:

1. Vulnerability is more than disclosure.
2. Vulnerability inherently comes with risk, so don't wait for it to feel easy. It never will.
3. Vulnerability must be practiced safely in an incremental way in conjunction with Consistency.
4. Vulnerability should start with, and lead back to, Positivity.

Do we want a workforce that is creative, proud, authentically expressed, and diverse? Do we want a team that values one another, solves problems together, apologizes appropriately, and takes greater risks? Do we want to feel as accepted in our failure as in our success? Do we want to belong even if we don't fit in? Do we want to believe we'd be supported if we go through a personal crisis?

Please say yes. I know it's scary to think of "adding more Vulnerability" into our work, but all that really means is asking us to show up with courage, openness, empathy, and curiosity—things we already possess. Vulnerability isn't "adding more" of something as much as it's a refusal to keep asking us all to pretend that "less is better." Compartmentalizing us doesn't work. Fully human is who we are. Fully human is what our workplaces need.

We can *see* each other in safe and satisfying ways.

THREE WAYS TO INCREASE VULNERABILITY

1. **Engage in "Small Talk" with New People.** Few of us love trying to make conversation with people we don't know well, and yet it's the currency of connecting. It'll be hard to get to meaningful stuff if we have nothing to build upon. So have a couple questions in your repertoire: an easy one: "So what did you do this last weekend?" a favorite one: "What got you into this profession?" as also, as perfectly suggested in an op-ed titled "The Awkward but Essential Art of Office Chitchat," practice turning the "how are you" question into a conversation by sharing *why* you're good: "I'm good. I just started a book/podcast/TV show and I'm really enjoying it. Have you heard of it?" Or mention something office-related, a shared common experience: "I'm good. They restocked the cold brew in the kitchen and it's so strong. Have you tried it?"[8]
2. **Clarify What We Need.** Let's tell someone what would be more meaningful to us or what behaviors we'd prefer. Instead of stewing, complaining, or venting, think of a situation in which we can try to practice telling someone what would feel better to us going forward.
3. **Focus on Highlights and Lowlights for Deepening the Relationship.** My favorite question with friends is to ask them to share one current success in their life and one challenge. This week at lunch, ask a friend to share how she'd answer that question!

THREE WAYS FOR MANAGERS TO INCREASE VULNERABILITY

1. **Facilitate Personal Sharing.** Maybe it's gathering everyone up on Monday morning to check in with one another over coffee for twenty minutes, or paying for a weekly lunch when everyone eats together, or allotting some of our time during team meetings—whenever the time is, use it wisely for the purpose of some personal disclosure. Sample questions are available at www.thebusinessoffriendship.com.
2. **Encourage Pride.** We all crave feeling proud, and yet we often feel guilty for feeling it; so let's help our team boost their confidence and normalize how important it is for us to take pleasure in our accomplishments. We'll look for opportunities to tell them when we're impressed with them, we'll ask them to tell all of us what they're doing this month that leaves them feeling the proudest, and we'll help facilitate them in expressing when they see the accomplishments and contributions of one another.
3. **Name the Uncomfortable.** It's easier to justify and make excuses, to look the other way, and to hope that conflict and hard emotions simply resolve themselves. But we'll see those as opportunities for us, and our team, to practice our Vulnerability. Then we'll be the ones to ask, "What are you feeling right now?" when we sense a mood shift; "Is everything okay between you two?" when we pick up on tension; "What do you need right now to feel peace again?" when we know someone is stuck; and "What's the hardest part of this for each of you?" when the team is facing an obstacle.

PART 3

How to Make Relationships Work Better for Us

Healthy Goals and Expectations for Relationships at Work

Do We Have to be Friends With Everyone?

Now we know that all relationships start at the bottom of the Triangle with only some relationships progressing up the peak toward Frientimacy as we practice the Three Requirements, but now let's look more closely at *how* that works.

Better understanding exactly how we increase our closeness to someone gives us powerful information for more intentional influencing, bonding, connecting, selling, leading, and collaborating. It also provides us with a framework for better understanding what level of relationship we have with any one person and establishes healthier expectations of what actions are appropriate.

Basically, there are three powerful questions we have in every relationship:

1. Currently, where on the Triangle is this relationship based on how much we're practicing the Three Requirements?
2. Then, are my expectations and actions an appropriate reflection of our actual relationship (as opposed to acting like we're at the top or bottom when we aren't)?
3. Finally, where do I want this relationship to be? Do I want to maintain it where it is, develop it up the Triangle to feel closer, or lessen this relationship (or my expectations) toward the bottom of the Triangle?

How we practice the Three Requirements will look different based on where we are on the Triangle with someone *and* where we want to be with someone.

In other words, it's not just friendships that aren't all or nothing; neither are the Three Requirements. It's not "Should I be vulnerable with this person?" as much as "How much should I be vulnerable with this person?" It's not "Should I be kind to this person?" as much as "How much Positivity—affirmation, laughter, joy, expressed gratitude—is appropriate in this relationship?" It's not "Do I trust this person?" as much as "What specifically should I trust this person to do or not do?"

Obviously, the way we interact with strangers, social media followers, office bullies, and onetime customers at the bottom of the Triangle should look different than how we interact with our good friends at work, our favorite vendors, and our lifelong clients, who might be in the middle of the Triangle. Likewise, there should be a marked difference between how we interact with those in the middle of the Triangle, no matter how close we feel to them, compared to our closest intimates, confidantes, and lifelong friends who might be at the Top of the Triangle.

But before I show you how to move people up and down the Triangle (and most importantly, how to move your expectations to match the level of relationship you *do* have, not the one you *want to* have), let's look at the five levels of the Triangle where all our relationships reside.

THE FIVE LEVELS OF RELATIONSHIP

By now, hopefully, it's abundantly clear to all of us that all relationships are on a spectrum. To provide us with a visual, I'm adapting some of my previous work to illustrate the various levels of all relationships, starting at the bottom of the Triangle where all relationships start.

Level One: Curiosity

Curiosity is the floor, the very bottom, of how, hopefully, we interact with people. Here's where we practice the lowest level of Positivity with *kind actions*, the lowest level of Consistency with *reliable interaction,* and the lowest level of Vulnerability with *genuine interest* appropriate to that context.

Hopefully we are friendly, committed to giving whatever time and attention is appropriate, quick to introduce ourselves, willing to share a little, and interested in the other. This is where all healthy relationships start. We're curious about getting to know each other, eager to learn what makes each other unique, and prepared to show up with respect.

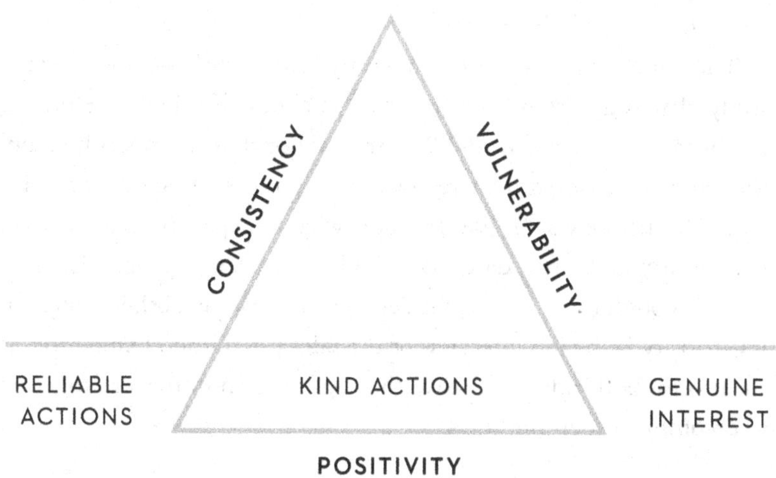

Our nonverbal body language is crucial at this early stage—people are asking, "Is this person warm? Are they likable?" So we will practice maintaining eye contact, giving sincere smiles, nodding our head, and keeping our body language inviting and open. We hope our body matches our words in communicating "I'm interested in finding out more about you." In fact, while we want to be appropriately open with what we share with someone, we will have far greater success in connecting with them by focusing more on what's likable about them than in trying to be liked.

Without a doubt, the largest quantity of our interactions is at this stage. And the majority of them will stay here.

Level Two: Exploratory

But with some—because there was enough Positivity, Consistency, and Vulnerability that left us leaning in, open to more, or interested—our relationship can move into the second phase of exploration as we move up the Triangle. At this level, we increase our Positivity as we look for things we like about each other and find ways we might enjoy each other; we increase our time together to better find out who we each are on a more Consistent basis; and we increase our Vulnerability a bit by showing genuine interest in learning about each other and revealing parts of who we are.

This phase in a relationship typically lasts a while—remember the study that suggests it takes most of us about fifty hours before we might feel like we're friends? Whether or not those numbers hold up, the truth is that even if we're both gung ho, it still takes a lot of interactions before we feel like we know what to expect from each other. If Curiosity is the first date, then Exploratory is two people deciding there's enough there to warrant getting to know each other more. Or, if Curiosity is the job interview or the sales pitch, then Exploratory is the process both sides agree to as they figure out how to work together to accomplish their purposes.

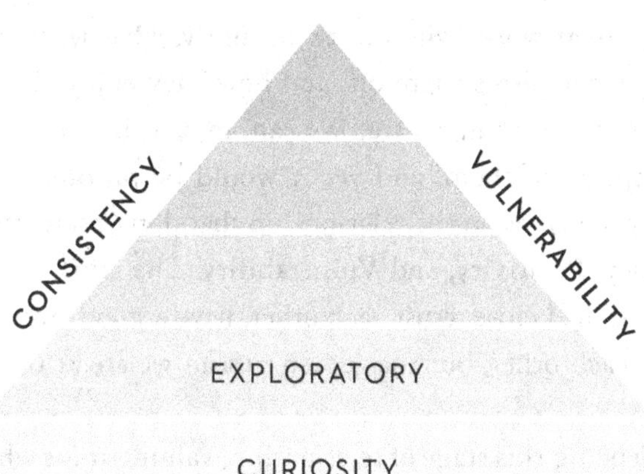

This stage is where the vast majority of the people we know and interact with somewhat regularly will reside. For many, our relationships with them will forever stay here as we may never feel like our relationship has a strong pattern of Consistency that leaves us feeling all that close. We can stay here and acknowledge that we will need to show up with each interaction looking for clues as to how we can best be reliable (Consistency), kind (Positivity), and honest (Vulnerability) in this specific context.

Level Three: Familiarity

Once we start feeling closer—like we can better predict how that person will respond or what they might choose in this situation—we have stepped into the next phase of Familiarity. We're now in the middle of our Triangle, so we've come a long way from our "minimum expectations," which means we might be more generous with our time, more honest with our stories, and quicker to know how to have fun together. But it's important to note that just as there are two levels we've traversed, there are also two levels still higher.

It's at this stage that we can sometimes start getting ahead of ourselves. We can mistakenly think that because we are *familiar* with how they are at work, who's in their family, what they did over the weekend, what pisses them off, and how they enjoy their free time that we are closer than we are. We can, in fact, be *very* familiar with certain aspects of them, and yet it would be problematic to place higher expectations on the relationship that don't match the levels of Consistency, Positivity, and Vulnerability. The truth is that at this level we can feel close, trust each other, have a good time, and genuinely like each other, but that doesn't mean we are at the Top of the Triangle.

Experiencing this stage of relationship, valuing it for what it is, can be the difference between loving our work and not. We don't feel like we're still trying to figure each other out, we feel safe asking questions, we have some history behind us, and we've made some good memories along the way. We hopefully feel accepted for who we are at work, validated for what we bring, and supported when we need it. While it's not a realistic expectation that all of our relationships with all of our coworkers will reside here (most of them may stay in Curiosity and Exploratory), we can absolutely develop at least a couple of them to this point, and the healthiest of teams will have many relationships at this level.

Some people don't want to move their work relationships up higher. That's fine, but in that case, make sure you are diligent about fostering other nonwork friendships in your life (that is, making the time outside of work to keep up with them consistently) that do fill the Top of your Triangle. Too much of our loneliness comes at this point when we realize that we have few, if any, relationships that go any higher. Too many of us have social groups, or *familiar* friends, and yet we still don't have a chosen few, or anyone really, who truly *sees* us in more than one role, context, or place.

Level Four: Commitment

Hopefully a handful or two of our relationships will eventually develop into the next level of Commitment. They move here because we have intentionally upped our game in how we practice the Three Requirements.

At this stage we are *committed* to practicing our Consistency in new and extended ways. This means, among other things, that we're taking responsibility for spending time together, not just seeing each other at work. We're inviting each other to things, introducing each other to other people in our lives, and spending time together in new contexts—whether that be the golf course, our backyard, or a favorite restaurant. We feel more responsible for each other's well-being and happiness as our commitment to our relationship increases. We have a history of being reliable and we have a future when we expect it to continue. Even past our job. (Any relationship before this level has a high likelihood of not surviving beyond our joint employment, as our Consistency was more limited to our work hours.)

At this stage we are *committed* to practicing our Vulnerability in broader and deeper ways. This means we're taking a few new risks to share and learn new things about each other—we're initiating conversations about things that matter to us, we're following up on things told to us the last time, and we're getting to know the other person in various contexts. Now we don't just know him as the brilliant computer engineer who we appreciate working with, but we are seeing a whole new side of him as he chases his kids around the pool and kisses his husband who's at the barbecue on their deck. Now she's not just our best friend at work who tells us about her love of art, but we're seeing finished pieces in her home and listening while she describes what they mean to her. We are seeing these people in new ways, watching them handle disparate experiences, and witnessing more of the myriad of their identities.

At this stage we are *committed* to practicing our Positivity in more expressive and generous ways. This means we're not worried about what they'll think of us when we tell them how much we respect or adore them. We're excited to pick out a thoughtful birthday gift for them because we feel like we know them better. We're hopefully practicing some platonic physical touch—showing that we're comfortable in their presence and feel warmly toward them. We are adding to the list of things we enjoy doing together, banking good memories, and taking photos because we want to remember.

This level of friendship is so meaningful, so soul-full, so comfortable. We *like* these people, not because they're the best people we've ever met, but because we feel seen in a safe and satisfying way. We trust them, we enjoy them, and we know them.

If we have these friends in our lives—whether it be two or six—we feel rich with relationships and can trust that if we needed them, they'd want to be there for us. This is a level that too few of us have, and yet all of us need.

Level Five: Frientimacy

And then there's the highest level—the Top of the Triangle—where we don't have to just hope that people would be there for us if needed—we've already proven it. These are the people with whom we've invested those "two hundred hours." Here, we are practicing the highest levels of the Three Requirements. Hopefully our spouses or life partners are in here (only by practicing the Three

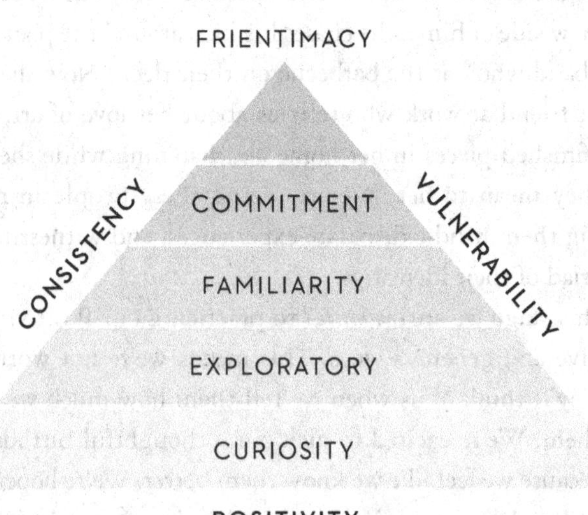

Requirements, not simply because we have a certificate!). But so, too, should there be a handful of others with whom we have platonic intimacy, or Frientimacy. These are our most trusted confidantes, our emergency calls, and the people we hope to keep in our lives for the long haul, if not forever.

But we don't just get here by really, really, really liking each other. And we don't just get here because of a couple long confessional sessions. And we don't just get here because one of us showed up in a beautiful way when we were in need. And we don't just get here because we work together and tell each other what's going on in our daily lives. No, we get here because we have both proven to show ourselves willing to completely take off our masks with each other—telling each other anything, because we've both reliably shown up in as many areas of each other's lives as possible, and because we've both been as generous as we could be to accept and love the other person as unconditionally as we possibly can.

When we get here, we are not just *updating* each other on stuff, but we're *processing* stuff together. If updating means revealing or informing about things going on in our lives, then processing means finding out together how we feel about it, what we're going to do about it,

COMPLETE ACCEPTANCE

SECURE COMMITMENT

MEANINGFUL TRANSPARENCY

CONSISTENCY

VULNERABILITY

POSITIVITY

and letting the other person influence that process. We're asking huge questions with each other because we trust the mirror, the cheerleader, and the intention of the other person.

And, importantly, here we very much acknowledge that we *are* a relationship. We aren't only two people in a relationship. Rather, we have this third entity of who we are together that we talk openly about. We share when our feelings are hurt, we whisper what we hope the other person can help us with, and we delight in sharing the side of us that only they can bring out.

Here, this is a relationship we're absolutely committed to not only maintaining but to protecting and building. We will pay money to go visit each other should we move away, we will absolutely be at the big events in their lives, and we will initiate calling them with our big news rather than waiting until the next time we catch up. These are our intimates—the closest of the close.

We can see both how wonderful it is to have people like this in our lives and how much one needs to invest to build the relationship that can live up to this. For at the Top of the Triangle, we have *secure commitment*, the highest expression of Consistency; *complete acceptance*, the highest expression of Positivity; and *meaningful transparency* in all areas of our lives, the highest expression of Vulnerability.

THE HEALTHIEST OF EXPECTATIONS

I share these spectrums and levels with you for a variety of reasons that mostly center on developing healthy expectations of what your relationships at work are, and what they are not. Here are three big takeaways I hope you picked up:

1. **Most of our work relationships will probably be on levels one to three.** That means we will be as genuine, kind, and reliable as we are able. We realize that someone doesn't need to be Top of Triangle to be meaningful,

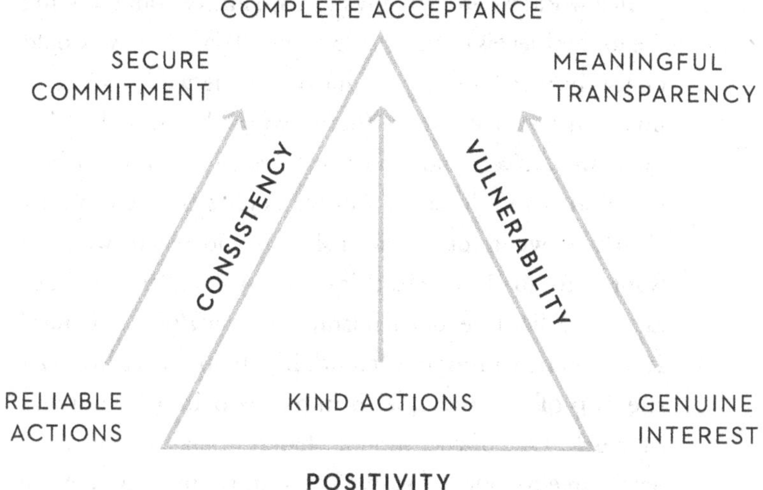

helpful, or enjoyable to us. We can seek to make any relationship as healthy as possible at these levels.

2. **We can feel close to, or familiar with, someone at work and that doesn't mean we have practiced Frientimacy.** This one understanding alone would save so much heartbreak. If our relationship is honestly at level three—mostly taking place at work, mostly centered on enjoying each other, and mostly dependent upon updating each other—this is not someone with whom we should expect to act like they are at levels four and five.

What ends most friendships isn't a betrayal of our friendship but a betrayal of our expectations of that friendship. In other words, we get our feelings hurt because the other person didn't act like the friend we wanted her to be, then we take that personally and tell a story about her not caring or being selfish, and then we are tempted to conclude she isn't a good person. But the truth is that such people may be amazing level-three friends whom we were hoping would act like level five. That doesn't mean they aren't good friends as much as it means we need to build a better friendship.

In a world where so many of us are lonely—and missing the highest levels of friendship on our Triangle—we would be forgiven for wanting to move anyone we felt close to into that vacancy. But it doesn't work that way. Just because we *need* a friend, and just because they *are* our best friend at work, doesn't mean we don't still need to look clearly at where our relationship is and where we both want it to go. To be clear: it's not "Are we friends?" but rather, "What level of friendship are we *really* practicing?"

3. **If we want to move a friendship from work toward the Top of the Triangle, it happens primarily outside of work.** One of the biggest changes that happens from level three to four is that we begin initiating new ways of being together outside of work. We begin to glue a new piece of our lives together—practicing an additional pattern of being together. This not only helps us get to know people in the other parts of their lives, but it ensures our friendship has a structure to rely upon, even if one of us changes jobs. This also means that most of the Vulnerability, Positivity, and Consistency that comes with levels four and five happen outside of work—we aren't sitting at our desks processing our lives.

Up to this point we've been learning about how to develop relationships in general, and mostly on teams. This final part of the book, Part 3, is all about how we can practice better friendships through our fears, unmet expectations, and with the most challenging of people and the most difficult of circumstances. Are you ready for the nitty-gritty? We're starting with that annoying coworker!

Reducing the Impact of "Toxic" Coworkers

Two Ways to Respond to Unhealthy Relationships

That knot in your stomach, that catch in your throat, those tears in your eyes, that pent-up anger—we know what it feels like to come home drained by someone at work.

Stories abound of coworkers who belittle, criticize, intimidate, undermine, dismiss, bully, shame, gossip, sabotage, and ostracize. Abound so much, in fact, that Dr. Mitchell Kusy's research for his book *Why I Don't Work Here Anymore* shows that 94 percent of the leaders he's surveyed concede they've worked with a toxic employee in the last five years. As he says about toxic employees: "Almost no one has been immune to the devastation they have wreaked on individuals, teams, and organizations."[1]

Devastation, indeed. Christine Porath, a Georgetown University professor of management, and Christine Pearson, professor at the

Thunderbird School of Global Management at Arizona State University, conducted a study of 14,000 CEOs, managers, and employees that shows just how much "incivility demoralizes people." When we feel stuck with a toxic employee on our team:

- 80 percent of us lose work time worrying about the offending behavior,
- 78 percent of us say our commitment to our organization declines as a result of that experience,
- 66 percent of us believe it hurt our performance and productivity,
- 63 percent of us lost work time trying to avoid that person,
- 25 percent of us admit to taking our frustrations out on our customers, and
- 12 percent of us end up leaving our jobs as a direct result of the uncivility.[2]

There is no doubt that those numbers cost us and our organizations dearly. Part of what excites me about teaching healthy relationships in the workplace is the hope that, with better training, we might inspire better behaviors in those around us. But if nothing else, the rest of us can learn how to protect ourselves as much as we can from those whom we feel are toxic.

WHO IS A TOXIC PERSON?

To be clear up front, I'm not a fan of the word *toxic* when it comes to labeling people. I've begrudgingly used the word sparingly because it's so ubiquitous in our culture, but calling someone toxic can be problematic, for many reasons, including:

- **It's too powerful.** The very word *toxic* communicates something poisonous—often synonymous with lethal, noxious, and fatal. To tell our brains that someone around us has that kind of inherent and pernicious power is enough to cripple any of us with a sense of defeat. None of us *really* wants to simply be a victim.

- **It's lazy.** If we don't like a behavior, we simply call it toxic and feel justified believing it's all *their* fault. One study of 22,000 people revealed that about 80 percent of us claim we've had a toxic friend at some point, with one in three admitting it had been their best friend.[3]

  What do we consider toxic? The top five most common answers were friends who 1) are self-absorbed, 2) are negative, 3) are critical, 4) gave backhanded compliments, and 5) were flakey. I'm not condoning any of those behaviors—they're obvious breakdowns of the Three Relationship Requirements. But who are we, all the nonpsychologists in the world, to be giving everyone who does one of those things—which we, ourselves, do—that kind of a terminal diagnosis? Remember, with 80 percent of us admitting this, it means we've either all been friends with the same 20 percent of toxic people out there . . . or chances are high that one of our friends considered us the toxic one. It's an awfully big and lazy word for actions that annoy us, personality differences we judge, or narratives we might mistakenly ascribe to their choices.
- **It's frequently not accurate.** If I had been surveyed if I'd had a toxic friend, I'd have said yes. Someone I used to be friends with immediately comes to mind. Yet she has a huge group of other girlfriends who apparently aren't dying in her presence. And, truth be told, she and I had a meaningful relationship for quite a time, too, before it felt dysfunctional. So did she suddenly turn toxic? And only with me? Instead of calling my friend toxic, it would have been more accurate to say our relationship started to feel toxic. That difference—putting the focus on our broken and hurtful pattern, our current experience instead of her as a person—reflects reality better.

> While there may be some psychopaths and other people walking around out there that nine out of ten of us, and some trained professionals, would agree qualifies as "toxic," the truth is that when most of use that word, it says less about the other person and more about the relationship we've developed with them.

To that last point, one of the questions each person on a team is asked on their *Healthy Team Relationship Assessment* is, "Is there anyone on your team who you feel consistently damages the overall relationship of your team?" Only about 10 percent of teams unanimously answer yes that there is indeed a toxic person. That means that the person *we* think is damaging the team only has a one in ten chance of being perceived that way by everyone else on our team. The vast majority, 70 percent of teams, are divided in their opinion. In fact, the people saying yes are usually in the minority. This by no means justifies damaging actions; nor does it mean that a manager shouldn't be concerned to have team members perceiving that there's someone damaging the dynamics. But it should humble most of us to realize that our assessment of someone is far from cut and dry, and that it is possibly less about *them* and more about *our relationship with them.*

For these reasons, I think we have more to gain by calling them toxic behaviors, actions, patterns, relationships, and dynamics, than we do in calling a person "toxic." Again, that's not to say there is no one out there who is toxic, but the power in shifting the focus is that while we cannot change people, we *can* change patterns, interactions, and relationships. A pattern requires at least two people, so assuming *we're* willing to try something different—even if it's to set up boundaries—we have already proven we can change the relationship in some way. Let's hold some humility that we aren't the final arbitrator of people, leave some space to believe we have some power in this situation, and grasp at hope that maybe, just maybe, we can protect our health and joy even in the presence of those whose actions exhaust us. As someone who is unusually sensitive to the energy of those around me, I fully understand that this is very difficult.

Before moving on, let's perhaps also see toxic behaviors as a spectrum. Just as trustworthiness isn't all or nothing (and considering one person can feel one way and someone else can feel differently about someone), it might be helpful to recognize there is a range of disruptive actions. Someone talking nonstop all day long might exhaust us, but we'd hopefully all agree that is mildly disruptive compared to more severe actions, such as humiliating someone in public, verbal abuse, spreading malicious rumors, or sabotaging someone's work. Yes, there are some relationships that drain us, some people who are immature, and some dynamics that feel dysfunctional. But is it possible that they aren't inherently evil, malicious, and out to kill us all? Can we make room for the belief that just because someone annoys us, or even disappoints us, doesn't mean we can't shift that dynamic?

This isn't to say that any of it should be ignored or is acceptable, but it is to clarify that the best response to one offense isn't the best response to another. If you're reading this and are suffering abuse, shaming, hostility (passive or aggressive), harassment, or sabotage in your workplace, this chapter is not for you. The healthy response to severe inappropriate behaviors is to remove yourself from the situation. Whether that's talking to your supervisor about having the abuser fired, reaching out to HR about being reassigned, or quitting your job—your safety, physically and emotionally, is of paramount concern.

This chapter is also not for those of us who supervise someone we consider toxic. That is a whole separate book, my friends. What I can say is that toxic behavior is contagious and demoralizing, and there is absolutely no reason for any of us to make excuses for them, put up with it as is, or look the other way—no matter how much we like them, how charming they appear to be, how smart they are, or how much money they bring in. If a manager can see glimpses of it, or even sense it, they can assume that is only the tip of the iceberg of what their team experiences. Chances are high that with managers this person is on better behavior when they're around and treats them with more respect than others. A manager has a simple choice, from my vantage point: address the problem with an attempt to repair the behaviors and rebuild trust with the team or, if that doesn't work, fire them. It's your job to protect your team, their energy, and their engagement at work.

With those caveats, this chapter *is* for those of us who can't fire the offenders, want to try to keep working where we are, and who also would very much like to minimize the worry, stress, frustration, and irritation that we feel with some of our coworkers whose behaviors are disrupting our energy, health, joy, and productivity.

RESPONDING TO TOXIC RELATIONSHIPS

In our personal life, outside of work, we have the option of ending a relationship with people whom we feel are toxic. As I said earlier, I think we do it all too often, and too easily. Nonetheless, we absolutely can drift apart, say no to invitations, and break up with them. That is a choice most of us don't have when we're at work. We might still have to work the same shifts, answer their emails, and even collaborate on projects. We don't have the luxury of avoiding them just because we dislike them, and this can be tough. (In Chapter 12 I give advice in case you get in a fight with a friend at work.)

The alternative then for most of us is simply to put up with it. We swallow our feelings, make excuses for their actions, and convince ourselves to just "be nice." Some of us feel guilty for being annoyed, feel pity because we know how much they need us, or feel shame because we don't think we're worth more. We mistakenly think that maturity means going along silently for the ride. And it's killing us. Literally.

Being in stressful relationships wears and tears our body, exhausts our minds, and saps our energy. One long-term study followed more than ten thousand subjects for an average of 12.2 years and, unsurprisingly, discovered that subjects in negative relationships were at a greater risk for developing heart problems (including a fatal heart attack) than those whose close relationships were not negative.[4] Another study, from UCLA, found that those with negative social experiences had higher levels of proinflammatory proteins that could lead to depression, hypertension, atherosclerosis, coronary heart disease, diabetes, and cancer.[5] Our immune system is weakened, our blood pressure increases, and stress wreaks havoc on our bodies. Maybe we could compensate for the stress if this were just one neighbor we had to interact with occasionally or a client we only have to talk to once a year, but when it's someone we work with regularly—it's simply not worth the constant and ongoing hit to our health.

Putting up with something, as is, is not maturity, it's fear. Fear of confrontation, fear of powerlessness, fear of being misunderstood, fear of not being liked, fear of change, or fear of being seen as too ________ (mean, sensitive, bitchy). Pick your word but accept the truth. Our muscles are weak at repairing relationships. Most of us will do everything we can to avoid any confrontation.

So here we are with someone who annoys us beyond belief—whom we can't just walk away from, but neither does it feel healthy and good to keep going as it is now.

What do we do?

Do you remember our five levels of relationship we discussed in the last chapter? That can serve as a visual illustration of the two options we have left to us at work.

Option One: Try to Repair the Relationship

No one is going to cheer for this option. But before you jump to option two—which moves someone down to the lowest level on our Triangle—I'd like to first suggest *trying* to stabilize the relationship at level two or three, depending on the relationship. I'm not advocating that you two need to someday become close friends or have any desire to move them up the Triangle. Repair, in this case, simply means making it the healthiest—least painful, highest performance—that it can be. The truth is that we stand a chance at making this relationship not only survivable but possibly even functional at level two, and maybe someday level three.

Level two, Exploratory, acknowledges that we do have some Consistency with these people since we work with them all the time and

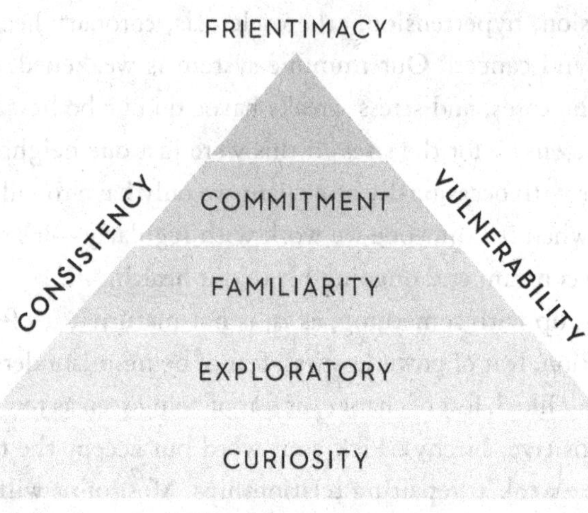

suggests that we first attempt to boost Positivity and Vulnerability to try to bring a better balance to our interactions. Choosing to try to fix, or strengthen, the relationship here means being very clear that we are *exploring* ways to get along better.

To be clear, we don't need to be convinced *they're* worth our effort or deserving of our exploration. We're going to try to repair this relationship for *our* sakes. Because we want to protect our health. Because we want to reduce our worry and frustration. Because we want to enjoy work a little more. Because we want to feel engaged on our team and in our organization. And because we value our personal growth.

Now, chances are high that Positivity is in poverty in this relationship. Which then begs two possible courses of action:

1. Figure out how to increase the positive feelings, and/or
2. Identify if there's any way to decrease the negative ones.

Our final path forward might include a combination of the two, but if we could determine even one conversation or boundary that we think might limit the negative, then our positivity-to-negativity ratio may not be as off balance as it is now.

Hugo couldn't stand how his boss micromanaged him. It made him hate her, he said to me, and it colored every interaction they had as he took her every question as evidence of her controlling nature. In this case, while finding things to laugh about together, celebrating wins, and complimenting her are all great acts of Positivity, they wouldn't be a drop in the bucket compared to his frustration. He had to figure out a way to decrease that negativity. In talking with him, outside of an off-site meeting where I was working with his team, we came up with the plan to have him practice enough Vulnerability to open a conversation with her to see if they could find a way through. At his next one-on-one with her, he shared, "There's something I'm hoping we can talk about because I want us to have the best working relationship possible. I frequently interpret your questions and actions as micromanaging me, which is leading to a lot of frustration that obviously isn't helpful. I guess I'm just wondering if I'm interpreting your actions wrong, if there's anything I'm doing to give you reason to doubt my abilities, or if there's anything we might be able to do going forward that helps both of us feel confident."

Now, not every conversation is going to be a home run, but in this case, Hugo was floored by her apologizing, her sharing with him how she was following what had been modeled to her, and her openness to hear what would feel better to him.

What he did so well was:

- start the conversation with his positive hope,
- take responsibility for how he interpreted the behaviors, which gave her the benefit of the doubt and lessened her need to be defensive,
- give an honest glimpse of the impact it's having on him, and then
- quickly turned it into a "how can we solve this together?" conversation.

But sometimes maybe it is as easy as finding more things to enjoy with this person, looking for things you admire, and forcing yourself to be more curious. Francine, a floor nurse, wrote me a message sharing, "There was this one guy in our department who I initially considered toxic because I felt like he was always judging me and making snide comments. It used to make me sick to my stomach to work the same shift with him." But one night, in the break room, instead of leaving when he came in, she decided to try to add Positivity through showing interest and asked him how he ended up becoming a nurse. His story resulted in her feeling some empathy and respect, but at the end of their short connection, he said to her, "You know what's funny is you're the only person here to ask me a question like that, and here I thought you were the intimidating one!"

"The intimidating one?" She was shocked, of course, and told him she had thought the same thing about him. They both laughed and talked about how easy it was to misinterpret each other's distancing as judgment, as opposed to the protection mode they both must have subconsciously taken around each other. She wrote me, "Now, I mean we're not best friends, but he's definitely an ally and someone I still love to joke around with in the break room. I actually feel like we have this bond, this secret understanding about each other that no one else knows." Francine didn't feel the negative was so bad that it initially needed addressing as much as she decided to lean into some Consistency—choosing to stay in the break room and interact—and some Vulnerability—asking a personal question and eventually being willing to share her own feelings.

Our goal is to figure out how we can decrease the negative feelings, whether that's with: setting boundaries, starting honest conversations, changing systems so we don't keep putting ourselves in the same situation, or choosing to practice forgiveness for the stuff we keep holding against them. And then we can be as generous and abundant as possible as we seek ways to increase the positive feelings. We aren't trying to fake ourselves out by plastering on fake smiles and dishing out insincere compliments. We are hopefully showing up and honestly asking, "How might the two of us experience some pride together? How might we share a moment of joy? What would it take to increase our hope, even just a little bit? Is there anything I can do to create any amusement for us?"

Usually, while it feels like the floor of Positivity has fallen out from under a relationship, or honestly was never there to begin with, we can't solve it without practicing Consistency and Vulnerability too. Truth be told, we might have more Consistency than we already want, but we might be surprised if we inquire:

- Are there any other ways we might interact other than how we do now?
- Should I try moving our communication to email for better clarity, or should I experiment with stopping at the person's desk to make a few minutes of face-to-face chitchat?
- Is it possible the person feels left out of important conversations or social events?
- Have I ever made myself available for a one-on-one conversation, or does it feel better if we interact more in a group setting to diffuse some of our dynamic?
- Is there anything I could do to be more consistent in the way I show up so they better know exactly what I expect or how I respond?

As for Vulnerability, while our goal isn't to confide in this person, there's no way to create a healthy relationship on the Triangle without taking some risks. If we want to try to create a healthy level-two relationship, since that's two-fifths up the Triangle, that would put our Vulnerability target between 20 and 40 percent.

- What can I do to help see this person better?
- What conversations might open us up a bit and remind us we're both human?
- What subjects seem to light the person up?

- Have I been honest with what I'm feeling or the impact that their behavior is having on me?
- If I needed to apologize for something, what might it be?
- What would it look like to try to say yes a bit more? Or are there places where I need to bravely say no?
- If there were complete honesty, what is one thing I might ask for that would make the biggest difference to me?

See what happens, if anything, if we give ourselves permission to be level-two friends. We can exhale and let go of any pressure to be more than that, and simultaneously we can acknowledge that the opposite of that isn't to be enemies. Sometimes once we have a better visual of what we're aiming toward, we not only can do a better job of contributing the right energy, but most importantly, we can establish better expectations. Which hopefully means a lot less future disappointment and frustration.

That's what happened for Karina. In her case, her "toxic friend" was actually the person she felt the closest to at work. They were similar ages, liked joking around, and seemingly became close as they saw each other every day for almost two years. But for as close as they felt, it was also her most stressful relationship. She believed her friend Jessica seemed set on competing with her. So much so that Karina felt that Jessica stole her ideas to look good in front of the boss, undermined her opinions in meetings, and unnecessarily criticized some of the ways she worked.

Now, if I were coaching Karina, because this was a relationship that felt important to her, I'd probably advise trying to open up a conversation with Jessica about these behaviors, since she claimed they were so close. I'd love for her to hear her friend's side of it—Does she feel insecure in her job performance? Does she feel like Karina is the one competing? Does she feel threatened by how their boss favors her? We won't know. It's possible they could have deepened their relationship had they tried. But, at minimum, realizing that they weren't as high up the Triangle as she thought they were, she was able to readjust, or

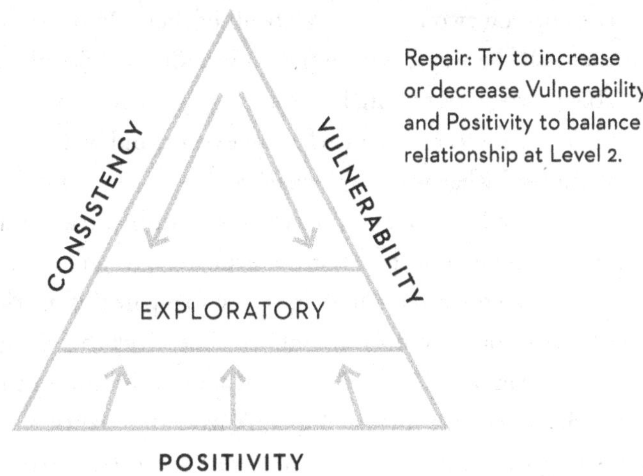
CONSISTENCY
VULNERABILITY
EXPLORATORY
POSITIVITY
Repair: Try to increase or decrease Vulnerability and Positivity to balance relationship at Level 2.

lower, her expectations. In this case, she actually needed to lower her Vulnerability to reflect that the relationship didn't really feel as safe as she wanted. It certainly didn't fix everything—there's far more she could have tried—but she said, "Honestly, just admitting she was a fun colleague, as opposed to my best friend, changed everything. It made me realize that I needed to invest in other relationships and to not be surprised that her work might sometimes matter more to her than our relationship. Which, if we're only at level three, makes sense to me! We weren't the best friends I wanted to believe we were."

Is repairing a relationship easy? Maybe not.

Is it awkward? Probably.

Is it good for us? Absolutely.

What possible actions can you experiment with to help balance out the Three Requirements in one of your relationships that isn't feeling healthy?

Option Two: Minimize the Relationship and the Expectations

But not every relationship can be saved, or needs to be.

If our first invitation is to try to bring all of the Three Relationship Requirements into better balance—possibly raising another one—

then option two is to deescalate all of them. In other words, we lower them all the way down to the bottom of the Triangle. And, as is true above, as we contribute less Positivity, Consistency, and Vulnerability, we also get clearer about what we expect, and what we don't, what we share, and what we don't, what we receive, and what we don't.

Louis, a line cook at a busy restaurant, had tried to play nice to all back-of-the-house staff, but unfortunately, he and the fry chef clashed, and he had no interest at all in trying to repair this relationship. He had a long list of grievances, ending with the belief that the guy "thinks he's better than he really is." He was all about minimizing this relationship.

But here's the kicker. We don't have the luxury of *not* having a relationship with the people we work with. By virtue of sharing the same space, time, and mission, we *are* connected. So this fry chef is still on Louis's Triangle. And fair enough if he decides he wants him as low as possible, but even at the bottom we are challenged to make our limited interaction clear and reliable (lowest Consistency), our actions kind and friendly (lowest Positivity), and our presence as authentic and curious as possible for our context (lowest Vulnerability).

As you can imagine, my opinion wasn't popular with Louis, but he begrudgingly admitted that it would feel better to at least have a slightly more amiable relationship. He refused all advice that had

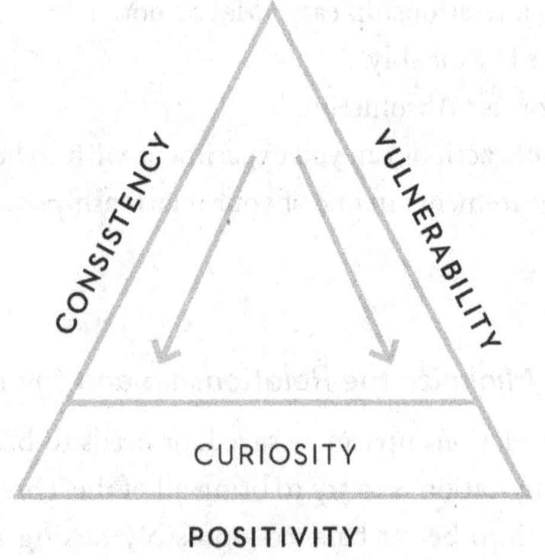

anything to do with the words "feelings, conversations, or apologies," but once he accepted that 1) they did work together and that 2) it "might as well be better," he went up to the fry chef the other night and basically said, "I know you don't really like me, and I sure as hell don't like you, but you have my word that while we're here at work I'll have your back." And apparently that did the trick. When he told me this story, I busted out laughing, but he did indeed show Positivity in affirming his support, Consistency in acknowledging that they both had to keep working together, and Vulnerability in admitting what they both felt. He said it released some tension, gave them something they could both agree on, and left him feeling more confident that neither of them would try to sabotage the other.

Maybe in our case it's not an arrogant coworker but a fussy client, a critical boss, a potential sales lead stringing us along, or an unknown social media follower. No matter who it is, at the bottom of the Triangle, we challenge ourselves to figure out how to treat them with the respect that prompts them, and us, to remember we are both humans. We don't have to volunteer more time than is necessary, share more than we feel comfortable sharing, or say a bunch of untrue niceties, but we do want to stay clear, kind, and curious.

Zachary, a vice president at a teleconferencing company overseeing operations, had to figure out what that looked like in his situation. The owner of the company had become increasingly distracted as he faced retirement, which meant a lot that needed to happen didn't. There was a lot of neglect and lack of resources. Zachary's frustration level was high by the end of nearly every day. His wife had to listen to him vent and rattle off all of the day's grievances. While this relationship had seemed good five years ago when he was first hired, now he felt as if he were hitting his head against a wall. He wanted as little to do with him as possible.

We separated out two things: 1) his work and 2) his relationship/expectations/feelings for this owner. With work—what absolutely needed to be dealt with and what strategies could he employ to make sure he could do his job around this owner? With the relationship—as we talked about lowering it, his shoulders sagged and he said, "The truth is that it's as low as it can go, but I'm doing two things wrong. One, I'm still acting like I expect him to act like the collaborator he used to be, so I'm constantly judging him and being frustrated. Two, because of that frustration, I'm passive aggressive and hardly what would count as kind, clear, and curious." Understandably, he needed to grieve that the relationship had changed, he needed to forgive the owner for caring less now, and he needed to simply expect the minimum. And then he needed to do what he could to make those minimum interactions as honest, kind, and reliable as he could so that his job would feel better.

When we're at the bottom of the Triangle with someone, we limit our interactions and shift expectations appropriately. We get clear on what we do trust in the other and what we don't. We try to empathize, validate, and appreciate when we can—and we take care of ourselves, adding in more joy with others. We courageously set boundaries and try to be as honest as feels safe in each encounter.

But above all, we remember that this stage is called Curious. In other words, we don't have to like them, but we'll do our very best to not create an unchangeable story about any person. We may keep our expectations low, but we'll always allow for them to surprise us with a random shared laugh, recognition that there's some things they do well, or the discovery that we have something in common.

And maybe they'll surprise us one day with not acting out in such toxic ways. But even if they don't, we can be proud of ourselves for showing up in the hardest of situations and practicing the most important of skills: being kind to people we don't like. The world is dying from lack of that. Thank you for being one more champion of civility—we need all the brave hearts we can find!

Increasing Belonging When We Feel Left Out

How to Respond to Cliques and Other Best Friends

"Thank God they were finally transferred to another department," a retail associate said to me about two colleagues who were best friends. When I asked what they did that was so destructive, she shrugged and said, "I don't know . . . it just bugged me that they were so close. It left me feeling like they had this loyalty to each other that would surpass their loyalty to any of the rest of us."

That can sum up how a lot of us feel when we're on the outside of a close friendship. It's not even that they did anything wrong as much as it's our fear that they might—that they might choose each other over their roles, over us, or over our shared goal.

Our last chapter was about how to reduce our interaction with people we don't like, but just as many of us have more angst because we feel left out or feel threatened by those who are closer to each other than we are to them.

NO ONE WANTS TO BE LEFT OUT

We are social creatures and we instinctually know that part of being in a relationship includes feeling chosen. Chosen because we have something to offer. It makes complete sense then that we'd want to be someone's favorite, that we'd compete to be seen as the best, and that we'd feel jealous if we felt like we were losing by some measurement.

Neuroscientists can now point to the part of the brain where we feel the pain of not being chosen, or of being excluded, and it won't surprise most of us to know it's the same part of the brain that processes physical pain. In other words, when we feel left out it displays in the same way as if we're kicked in the stomach. The pathology then isn't in feeling rejection, but in not. To feel it means our bodies are working the way they're supposed to—that pain is real.

Some of my favorite examples come from the research of Dr. Kipling D. Williams, a professor of psychology at Purdue University who studies such topics as ostracism, social conflict, and group conformity. His work repeatedly shows how ingrained our need to be included is—so much so that we show an outsized emotional response even when a computer game appears to favor someone else or leave us out. "The results have been remarkably consistent—within minutes of being excluded from the game, feelings of control, belonging, self-esteem, and meaningful existence are reduced."[1]

Those are no small feelings, and to ignore them risks us acting more irritable, expressing more anger, reporting greater depression, having higher rates of addiction, feeling less empathetic, judging more harshly, and experiencing more chronic physical illness.

His studies show that no matter our emotional health or personality, we all feel the pain. The difference between those who continue to suffer versus those who recover comes down to our ability to more quickly admit, "Oh I'm feeling left out." Then we can hopefully make the choices to respond in ways that reconnect us, as opposed to react in ways that further distance us.

And there's the rub. Because it's not the need for connection that causes drama but rather *how* we go about trying to meet this need. The drama we're so afraid of isn't from us needing each other as much as it's from how we might pursue feeling that connection in unhealthy ways and how we might behave when that need isn't met. We can recognize in ourselves, and others, what it looks like to chase that approval in unhealthy ways: never being able to say no, relying on false flattery, having to be right all the time, holding ourselves to perfection, overworking, or constantly managing our image—whether it's to be the funny one, the nice one, or the one to fear. Without often realizing it, we each default to a way of trying to win people over. Even pretending we don't care if they like us is simply the other side of the same coin—our way of protecting against rejection.

Unfortunately, when wounded or feeling left out, most of us default to irritation, blame, defensiveness, devaluing, and mean-spirited competition—all reactions that then tend to further our sense of disconnection as they decrease the odds of us feeling closer to others. Ironic, isn't it, that when our hearts and bodies call out for belonging, we are too often tempted to choose the actions that almost certainly assure us the opposite?

THE ANSWER: TAKE RESPONSIBILITY FOR DEVELOPING THE THREE RELATIONSHIP REQUIREMENTS

The healthiest response to feeling left out, then, is to ask, "What can I do to help foster more connection?"

The answer to jealousy, favoritism, or competition isn't to throw more blame on others for what *they* need to be doing for us. Rather, the answer is to take ownership of *our need* for connection by intentionally increasing the actions that lead to us feeling *seen* in *safe* and *satisfying* ways. In other words, building relationships up around us that increase Consistency, Vulnerability, and Positivity. We're working against our best interests when we resort to blame, defensiveness, and pouting. When we feel the threat of someone else getting something we want, it's our invitation to lean into the relationships that increase our chances of feeling included and valued.

This is some of the hardest work in the world to do because we fear that by leaning in more we'll only increase our feelings of rejection if it doesn't work, if we look like we care too much, or if we admit we want it. And I won't lie and pretend it's easy. It's most definitely the hardest work of humanity to stay open to love and connection when we feel scared, hurt, or unchosen. This is where the risk feels the greatest—to hold hope for more meaningful belonging when it feels in lack. But it's also the only way to ever get what we ultimately want because no one ever feels more connected by putting up their defenses and blaming others.

So what does it look like to lean into connection when we're hurt? It starts with us admitting that we'd rather feel closer and safer with some people, if possible, and then evaluating what we might be able to do to make that relationship healthier. Let's look at a few of the scenarios some of you shared with me and see if we can find a way through.

When Our Coworkers Seem to Have "Favorites" (aka cliques)

The fear of *the clique* has been with us since we were kids on the playground and continues to this day nearly everywhere people gather frequently—at the kids' school, in our neighborhoods, at our religious organizations, at association gatherings, and, yes, at work.

First, because we're prone to feel rejected even when no one is outright rejecting us, we have to answer honestly: Am I being blatantly "rejected" or is this an issue of me simply not feeling like I fit in? Neither is fun, but the difference is everything. In other words, are they telling us we can't join them, sending us away, or maliciously shutting us out? Or are they really just interacting and hanging out in such a way that makes us realize we aren't as close to them as they are to each other? Neither feels good, but if they aren't being malicious then by blaming them for our feelings of being left out, we're at risk of missing the invitation to build up our own connections.

The truth of the matter is that in most, maybe not all, but in most cases, what we're calling a clique is simply a couple of people who have more practice at the Three Relationship Requirements with each other. Meaning, they have probably known each other longer or they've had more opportunity to connect in different ways (Consistency), they may have some commonalities or went through some experience together that helped them feel seen by each other (Vulnerability), and/or they have had opportunity to really enjoy each other and feel good being around each other (Positivity). It makes complete sense that they gravitate to the people they have more relationships with—we do the same thing. The bummer is that, in this occasion, we don't feel close enough to them to gravitate. But that is not the same as saying they don't like us, wouldn't want to get to know us, or that they have no desire to include us. People feeling close to each other is not the same as people excluding us.

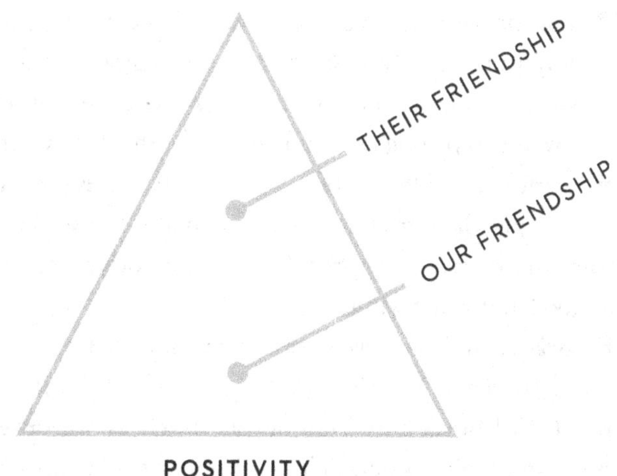

For David, he often felt left out by a group of execs who golfed all the time together. For Janet, it was watching a group of three women eat lunch together every day without them ever inviting her to join them. For me, it was joining a professional association "that felt cliquey" as I quickly sensed that there was a "hierarchy" of popularity, lots of inside jokes, and not a lot of people eager to connect with "the new person."

When we see a group of people who appear to be close, our temptation is to blame them for our not feeling included. But this is where the Triangle can be such a gift: it simply reminds us that some people are higher up the Triangle—not because we're not worthy or because they're exclusive but simply because they have developed a friendship. Our invitation is to:

1. **Be inspired.** While we hate feeling like we're on the "outside," it's always a good sign in any organization when you see evidence of good friendships—it means there are people who value it, know how to do it, and are practicing it. As hard as it may feel, it's a good sign of hope for us when we can look around and see that this workplace has fostered those kinds of connections. See it as a billboard of what's possible.
2. **Be compassionate.** We're at great risk of devaluing them or devaluing ourselves, so choose compassion as much as possible. Compassion for ourselves for the tender part of us that wants to belong and compassion for them for wanting the same thing. Neither of us is wrong. It makes sense that they enjoy their friendships *and* it makes sense that we want to experience that too. Try to hold both those truths as good and worthwhile.
3. **Be brave.** And then, we have to commit ourselves to practicing the Three Relationship Requirements knowing that we don't "break into" cliques as much as we develop friendships with people. This isn't a matter of auditioning

> for someone else to then choose us or invite us in. Rather, it's an invitation to consider how we can keep showing up, inviting others in, bringing joy to those around us, and choosing to stay curious as we express interest in others.

For David, he mentioned to one of the guys in the golfing foursome that he'd be happy to be a substitute if ever needed, but he also started asking around to see if anyone else wanted to get together to golf. He told me, "The biggest thing really was not taking it personally anymore. It makes complete sense to me, thinking about it now, that once they found a foursome that they'd want to play as much together as possible—not because they want to leave anyone out, per se, but simply because they've found a good thing and obviously they want to enjoy it. I don't begrudge them that. Honestly, if I had a great foursome going, I wouldn't be super eager to mess it up either or go through a bunch of work to mix it up!"

For Janet, she ended up feeling that the best way to build her connections wasn't to go insert herself in their time together, since they clearly looked like they had a lunchtime ritual down. Rather, she would start connecting more with each of the women one-on-one during the day. She said to me, "I just decided to take a more long-term approach and thought, 'If I regularly look for little moments to get to know each of them and leave them feeling even a little better after each interaction, then there's no way they won't eventually feel closer to me.'" True enough. She ultimately became really close friends with one of the women as they found some commonalities that opened up some meaningful conversations.

And for me, attending the professional association, I was tempted not to return since I hadn't felt all that included. But in taking my own advice, I figured I better commit to some Consistency on my part before I made that call. And sure enough, upon attending my fourth event, I found myself greeting people I recognized, having a conversation about getting more involved, and scheduling a lunch with a new friend. I also watched a new person look at me as though I were part of the "in crowd." Oh, the irony! We're all just wanting others to sweep us up and tell us we're accepted! I wanted it from others; she wanted it from me.

We are rubbing shoulders all day long with people who want to be accepted just as we do—even if they look like they don't. Our boss wants it. Those groups of friends want it. And we want it. What might change if we showed up judging everyone else a little less for how they're getting their needs met and focused a bit more on what we can do to build the relationships we want with everyone around us? I promise if you keep offering reliable interactions, genuine interest, and kind actions—you *will* bond people to you.

GOSSIP AND BETRAYAL OF SECRETS: HOW TO MINIMIZE BEING TALKED ABOUT BY OTHERS

But what if those people are talking about us? Or, more often the case, what if we fear that they are talking about us?

Let's be clear that this is a risk whether we have friends at work or not; and it probably lessens the more we like each other. But we definitely fear it.

Do an online search of "workplace gossip" and you'll get about ten million results in 0.67 seconds. Whether it's the fear of something we shared in confidence being told to someone else, or the fear of close friends judging us behind our backs—gossip, or even just the perception of it, destroys our hope of belonging.

In fact, I ask team members on the *Healthy Team Relationship Assessment* to score how true this statement is for them: "We have a no-gossip 'culture' that leaves me feeling confident that no one is talking about me, or others, behind our backs." And it gets the second lowest score of thirty statements. Too few of us are feeling safe. None of us likes the idea of being judged by others, but we like it even less if we feel we aren't there to explain, or defend, ourselves.

It would behoove our managers to bring this topic up and facilitate team conversations, asking questions such as, How do we define gossip? What protocol can we put in place that would leave us each feeling more trusting? What might our response be when we hear gossip? The managers can guide everyone through some possible scenarios and role-playing to help us practice responding in a nonshaming way to one another as we collectively relearn to interact without gossip, and to help us confront one another in constructive ways when we sense there might be some breach of our agreement.

But while most of us may not be able to set the tone for our workplace in a blatant way, we can most certainly allow the Triangle to guide us in such a way that we minimize our chances of being damaged by the insecurities of others:

1. **We focus on being known as ambassadors of Consistency and Positivity in our workplace.** The more consistent we are in our behaviors, the less people will believe anything that doesn't match what they've seen us reliably do; the more people enjoy being around us, the less people will be motivated to want to hurt us. It's to our benefit to build healthy relationships all around us so that those at work consider us their friends, or at least friendly.

   As such, when people around us gossip, part of being consistent and positive is to practice putting a stop to it as much as possible. Gossip isn't just an act of speaking but also an act of listening. Depending on the situation, sometimes just saying, "Oh I'm going to assume that person had good intentions," and trying to change the subject is enough, but other times we might have to deliberately call it out by saying, "I'm sure you don't mean to be gossiping, but have you talked to this person about this yet?" Or, "I feel uncomfortable talking about this person without them here—do you mind if we keep the conversation on x?" If anyone pushes back or tries to make us feel bad for not participating in the gossip, it becomes an opportunity to build trust with the gossiper by saying, "I hope you know I would do the same for you if I ever hear anyone talking about you."

2. **We follow the principles of Vulnerability—being thoughtful about slowly opening up in incremental and escalating ways.** As much as possible we filter what we share and do through the lens of "How safe do I feel with the people in this conversation?" Remember, the lower the Consistency or Positivity with someone, the lower our Vulnerability should be. We can always strive for authenticity in any specific scenario, but that doesn't mean we open up completely, share all our ideas and opinions, or disclose details if there are people we don't yet know, people we know who aren't reliable secret-keepers, or people whom we don't feel have our best interests in mind.

While there are no exact rules we must all follow, because our circumstances are all so different, let's look at an example of how slowly and incrementally we want to divulge anything at work that we fear might hurt us. Basically, how can we practice Vulnerability in a safe way that minimizes our chances of ever feeling like we're the subject of gossip. For an example, let's look at how we could potentially share our clinical depression with those at work.

With brand-new colleagues we don't know well, we might not even need to mention it, as we're looking to bring happiness to those relationships at the bottom of the Triangle, and authenticity doesn't mean that we need to tell everyone everything.

Maybe with a couple of coworkers or our supervisor, with whom we might be further up the Triangle, we could divulge more. To a trusted boss we might share, "I actually struggle with depression sometimes. I wanted to tell you because I may be taking a few mental health days here and there and I wanted to make sure you knew that it wasn't a reflection on how much this job means to me." Whereas, with a coworker, we might simply start with a question, "Have you ever had to take a mental health day or wished you could?" to help feel out how safe it is to confide. Or, in a team meeting, when we feel it's appropriate to what's being discussed, we might feel comfortable sharing, "I've actually been depressed before so I know a little about what our audience might be feeling in this situation." What's important in these settings is that while we might be revealing a new thing about us, we are doing so in a limited, thoughtful, and relevant way that communicates that we are taking care of ourselves.

Maybe, based on how they responded (empathy, validation) and how safe we feel over time after revealing what we shared (have they kept it secret? have they opened up a bit with us?), we might eventually feel close enough to someone to go into a bit more detail. Perhaps over a lunch or walk—away from our responsibilities—we might share a bit more about the impact it's had on us. But even here, if we're not Top of the Triangle friends who have a long history of being close in a variety of contexts, then we take responsibility to not lean on this coworker as our personal counselor. No matter how interested they are, we don't lay more on the relationship than the structure we've built so far can handle; and we make sure they also hear us describing all that we're doing to care for ourselves, the goals we have, and how much our work still means to us. We don't leave anyone at work wondering if we're capable of our job.

Then, ideally, we have a best friend or two, perhaps outside of work, with whom we can share the doubts, the fears, and the big feelings. If we don't have these relationships at the Top of the Triangle, we remain clear that it is not the responsibility, or fault, of the people at work to have to step into this role. It's our job to foster these friendships . . . and to hire the professional support we need alongside them.

It's wise in every relationship to slowly practice moving our Vulnerability up one notch at a time, but in a workplace setting it becomes even more crucial to build the mutual trust in each other incrementally.

3. **When we're the target, we move the relationship with the person who is gossiping to the bottom of the Triangle.** At minimum, this reminds us that they weren't reliable (Consistent), so we stop having expectations that they are to be trusted in the future, at least until proven otherwise. But this also means that we remember that we're still to treat them with the minimum of the requirements: still striving to be empathetic and respectful of their humanity (Positivity), someone they can rely upon to perform strongly during shared work projects and meetings (Consistency), and someone who will be brave enough to lean in and ask honest questions (Vulnerability).

The bottom level of the Triangle is Curiosity, which calls on us to be curious more than judgmental: we can try to assume the best, that this person wasn't trying to maliciously take us down as much as they were probably trying

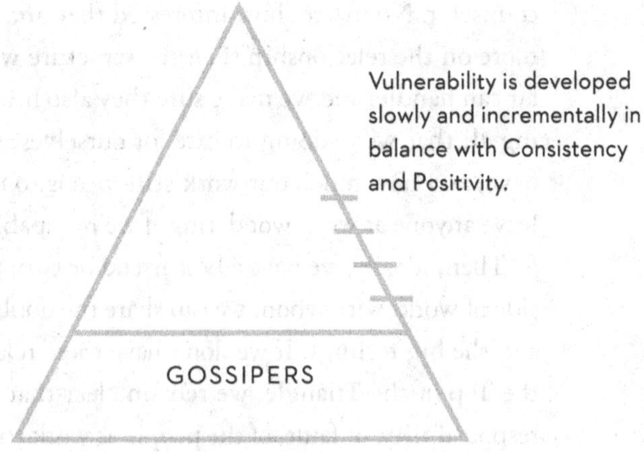
Vulnerability is developed slowly and incrementally in balance with Consistency and Positivity.
GOSSIPERS

to be seen as "someone in the know" or trying to feel like they "belonged." I always try to have as much compassion as possible for people who gossip, realizing that usually they simply want to look good to someone or feel connected (both good things we all want) but that they, unfortunately, don't always know how to do that well. It usually comes from a place of insecurity, or from feeling left out, and says more about them than it does about us.

But that's not to say we need to ignore it.

4. **Confronting those who might be gossiping about us is perhaps the most important expression of Vulnerability we can practice with them.** It will always feel hard to respond to the source of the gossip, but having a conversation might lead to them seeing the pain their gossip caused (the consequence of their actions for you), them understanding their risk of being seen as someone untrustworthy (the consequence of their actions for them), or even us better understanding the situation that was causing them to make assumptions. The initial goal, then, isn't as much to show up with fuel for them in the form of insults, judgments, assumptions, and more details, as much as it is to try to show up to take some of the fuel away with questions, curiosity, and a desire to build a stronger relationship.

   Depending on the situation, we can sometimes start with a "Hi, X. Can I sit down and talk to you for a moment? It's just recently come to my attention that you might have some questions for me about Y. And while it may not be appropriate for me to share all the details about it, I'd be happy to try to answer what I can. . . ." Then be quiet and see how they respond.

   Or if we haven't yet heard anything specific, but fear there's an issue, we can ask, "I wanted to take a couple of minutes and make sure things are okay between us. Sometimes I sense a little tension and I was wondering if you

> felt that too? Or if you had any idea what's causing that between us?" Other times we might need to be more blatant, all while trying to sidestep defensiveness and stay focused on problem solving: "Unfortunately I heard some mean things repeated about me, and while I'm sure you never meant to hurt me, I was wondering if you'd be willing to help me put this fire out?"

Our overall goals are to do what we can to not participate in gossip, to try to put a stop to gossip with kindness and clarity, and to practice being brave enough to go straight to the person we have a problem with, rather than respond the way the gossipers do by talking it out with everyone else.

WE CAN INCREASE OUR BELONGING

Whether we want to feel closer to others or simply hate the idea of others being closer than we are—the invitation is for us to ask: Do I feel like I belong on this team? If so, how might I help others feel included in that? And, if not, how might I intentionally lean in to the actions that might leave me feeling more connected, rather than more resentful, jealous, or begrudging?

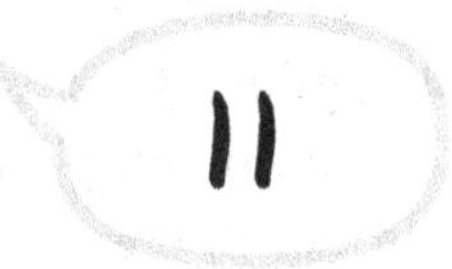

Fear of Favoritism, or Does It Have to Be Lonely at the Top?

How to Support Our Leaders Having Friends

"I've never been lonelier," Monica wrote me after a recent promotion at her financial institution. "I have more decisions to make than any other time in my career, and yet I feel like I can't talk it out with anyone. . . . Everything is so confidential or hard to explain. Add to that, I'm working longer hours so even my few friendships outside of work have taken a huge hit."

We frequently talk about how lonely it is "at the top," and yet we've almost resigned ourselves to believing that's the way it has to be. As a workforce we need to sit with that and inquire whether we really want to create a world where the people who are making the biggest decisions and casting the vision for the rest of us are being expected to do that from a place of disconnection and loneliness.

Not only do they need connection, but the sad reality is that most of them aren't getting it. Our leaders are lonely. One study a number of years ago suggested that 60 percent of CEOs say they're lonely and three-fourths of them say it's hurting their performance.[1] Extrapolate that to all managers, supervisors, and leads—and that's a big chunk of our workforce. If it's not social loneliness (from lack of interaction), then it's usually emotional loneliness (lack of closeness) or situational loneliness—triggered by not having people who really *get* what they are facing. The responsibilities and pressures they face, from themselves and others, makes them at risk of feeling distance between them and those around them.

OUR LEADERS NEED FRIENDS TOO

Our bosses, before they are their role, are humans, who just like us need to feel *seen* in a *safe* and *satisfying* way. They need connection as much, if not more, than the rest of us. The more stress we carry, the more we need supportive relationships to buffer our bodies from that impact. The less time we have for connecting is often a sign that we need it more than ever. Our bosses have a greater likelihood of being happier, connecting with our team more, and giving us more permission to have friends at work when they are also getting their needs met. We benefit from them having meaningful friendships.

One might push back and say, "Yes, well, I want them to care about their teams, but there's no need for them to be closer to some than others." Or one might give the traditional response, "Yes, but they can go make friends in mastermind groups or with other people at their level—just not someone who reports to them." That might work if we were all going to forever stay in the same positions and in the same companies, but as an administrator once told me, upon my asking why he treated all the interns with such respect, "Who knows . . . in ten years you could be my boss." In many ways it might be less messy to simply do a better job of training everyone on how to develop appropriate and healthy relationships than to ask people to keep switching who they can befriend every time there's an employment change.

To that point, look at the friendship of Jeff and Omar, who met at work twenty-five years ago when Jeff, who in an entry-level job at a telecommunications company, went into Omar's office, who was several levels above him at the time, and introduced himself by asking for advice on how to advance his career. Their friendship developed alongside their careers to the point where Jeff eventually reported directly to Omar. It was this "genuine friendship," he said, that was the hardest to leave a few years later when he accepted a position as COO for a start-up. Was that hard on the friendship? I asked, wondering if Omar had felt disappointed, betrayed, or hurt. "No, he totally understood it was too good of an opportunity to pass up." And they needn't have worried because over the years Jeff would work again for Omar at a different company, and at one point when Jeff was CEO at a software company, he recruited his friend to come work for him as VP. Roles completely reversed. And this time he beat me to the punch: "No, it wasn't hard. We could trust each other, we respected each other, and there was no one else I'd rather have working alongside me." They eventually started their own consulting company together, but more importantly they have maintained their friendship throughout their careers. Imagine if they had to stop their friendship every time one of them worked for the other.

Unfortunately, that's all too often what we expect. "I'm all about our employees having close friends at work," a human resources director for a global media company told me. "But where it gets too messy is if our supervisors try to be friends with their direct reports. That's where I draw the line."

ACKNOWLEDGING THE FEARS AND HESITATIONS

What are we afraid of?

All it takes is looking at the answers to "What are your biggest hesitations or fears about workplace friendships?" in general, and we quickly see that not only are three of the top five most popular answers directly related to that boss/employee relationship, but we also see what we're most afraid of, specifically:

1. *Risking favoritism* 42 percent
2. Betrayal of secrets/information 38 percent
3. *Needing to fire/reprimand a friend* 37 percent
4. *Maintaining friendship if one becomes boss* 30 percent
5. Losing the friendship after leaving the job 29 percent[2]

Those aren't small things.

But allow me to remind us that drama doesn't disappear simply by removing the word *friendship* from our leadership lexicon. It'd be one thing if all three of those risks—the appearance of favoritism, awkwardness around firing others, and transitioning to new reporting roles—were nonexistent in a company without friendship. But a workplace without friendship is hardly safe from these concerns. It's not a given that our supervisor won't still overlook our talents just because they have no friends on our team, that being fired by them is less painful if we don't feel like they care about us, or that reporting to someone we don't respect is more fun than if our friend were promoted.

Obviously, not a one of us wants to ever feel insecure in our jobs, underappreciated, or confused in our roles. I get that. Without a doubt, if we're human then we're prone to worry about not feeling as special as someone else. Double that worry if that someone else is also responsible for helping us earn a living. It makes sense that every insecurity button might get pushed if and when our boss appears to be closer to one of our coworkers.

But what if it's better relationships for them, not lack of them, that might lead to the stronger communication that is more likely to leave us feeling more seen in safe and satisfying ways?

RECOGNIZING THE BENEFITS AND POSSIBILITIES

I personally have yet to meet any leaders who, because of a meaningful friendship, stop caring about their team, their reputation, or their mission.

We're all too often setting them up for failure if we expect them not to bond with the people with whom they work. The very nature of their work has them practicing the Three Relationship Requirements regularly with the same people; there's really no way *not* to feel closer to each other if they're committed to being leaders who value the relationships around them. In fact, they're the ones who are most often scheduling and planning the very "team bonding" activities that we all hope will bring the team together, so it seems unlikely to expect the results to differ for them.

If we ask them not to feel closer to any one person than another, then we're asking them to only bond up to the level of the weakest relationship on the team. If we blame them for anyone who feels jealous or worried, then we are essentially not only blaming them for getting healthy needs met but also robbing the rest of us from doing the emotional growth that is ours to do. Our insecurities, discomfort, and fears will be there for us to examine and own whether our leaders have friends, or not—and, besides, we don't solve jealousy by taking something away from someone else.

The truth is that if we can't trust our leaders to want to still create as healthy of a team as possible, no matter who their friends are, then we have a serious leadership issue we need to address.

But fortunately, almost all of the leaders I interviewed argued that their friendships actually helped them better navigate these very tough scenarios mentioned above.

- **In avoiding favoritism:** "Because I was so sensitive to not wanting it to appear that I was giving preferential treatment to some of the people I was closer with on the team, I think it made me a better leader, because I ended up giving more one-on-one time to every person on my team. The more I got to know each team member, the better I could articulate their strengths and contributions, and the more they trusted my decisions. As long as they knew they were seen and valued, I never had any problems."

- **In firing a friend:** "I felt sick knowing I needed to replace my friend because she simply wasn't pulling her weight on our team. Of course, I've felt that way about every person I've ever had to let go. But, interestingly, because of our long-standing friendship, we were able to have a deeper conversation that led to her admitting that she really missed her past life as a dancer and how much she hated working in an office. In some ways, because of our friendship, it felt like I was actually better honoring her by encouraging her to not settle at this job."
- **In evaluating and giving feedback:** "I often joke that I wish I could schedule all my friends outside of work to come have 'employee evaluations' with me because they are so bonding. I trust the friendship I have with one of my employees more than I do any other friendship in my life because it's the only friendship where we've had to talk about our growth edges, where we want accountability, what boundaries we need to set, and what kind of support we each need from the other. I love knowing we are cheering the development in each other."

Obviously, those great examples aren't how it always goes down, but it's good for our minds to remember the potential and to consider better training our leaders on best practices. For beyond those three common fears, when I surveyed some of those who have loved having friends they report to, or vice versa, I heard all kinds of additional potential benefits too.

We learn from each other. An assistant editor credits her close friendship with her senior editor as the place where she's learned the most about what it takes to be in a similar role someday: "Seeing behind the scenes has helped prepare me more than anything for the kinds of decisions that must be made and the level of chaos I have to be ready to take on." But it goes the other way too. Several supervisors shared how much it has helped them to have someone they can trust on their team giving them honest feedback. A hospitality manager said, "It was my friend who was able to tell me how the waitstaff felt more exhausted than inspired by my attempts at leading cheers and getting everyone revved up for their shift. It immediately gave me permission to show up with more authenticity." Friends at work have a front-row perspective to who we are at work, and where we can grow, in a way that no other spouse, neighbor, or college friend can offer.

We feel less divided in our lives. This benefit—the feeling of support in having at least one friend who is familiar with both their personal and professional worlds—came up quite a bit in interviews. An art director shared how painful it was to lose her mother last year and how meaningful it felt to have at least one person at work knowing how torn up she was about the loss. "I mean, I told my team—so they knew, but it was such an anchoring feeling to have my friend there who *really* knew just hard it was for me. It made me feel a little less like I was hiding something or trying to pretend it didn't really matter." Joseph said something similar, but for him it was sharing the love of fatherhood with his regional coordinator, Bobby. He confided, "I often feel, as a guy, that we're not supposed to be that devoted to our kids. I rarely talk about my two boys as much as I sometimes want to. So I love that Bobby knows my kids, attends some of their parties, and thinks they're awesome. It helps me feel like even though I'm one of his sales guys, he also sees me as a father, which means more than I realized."

We can accomplish big things because of our shared trust. A common theme from those who have worked closely with friends is how much the friendship—because they knew each other's strengths and trusted each other—led to big things like changing the DNA of a team, coming up with a big idea, starting a new revenue stream, or taking on a challenging deadline. Matt hired one of his best friends to work for him after a frank conversation about what it would look like to supervise him. He concluded, "I honestly couldn't have created that department without him. It would have taken years to have developed that level of trust with someone else." When we care deeply for the person we're working for, or with, we're both willing to put in more hours, we're less competitive with our strengths, we feel safer to brainstorm big ideas, and we're more willing to take on a risk as we feel like we're not in it alone.

We take things less personally and assume the best more often. The closer we feel to someone, the less defensive we need to feel. We learn that that's just the way he reacts to stress and it's not about us, we're more willing to check our stories out with each other before jumping to conclusions, and we're less likely to get our feelings hurt when she doesn't respond in the way we hoped. The more we believe that people have our back and aren't out to hurt us, the more we are willing to trust their explanations and forgive their mistakes. Linda said, "Working for my friend for three years was the best job ever because we so easily gave each other the benefit of the doubt. It wasn't until then that I realized not only how much of my other jobs have lacked that but how much energy we spend because of that!"

Hearing some of the testimonies from others makes that clear line we often want to draw between friendship and leadership a little less clear, doesn't it?

But here's what hopefully feels a little clearer:

1. Friendships are happening—whether we want them to, or not. Even with our leaders.
2. Avoiding friendships doesn't automatically avoid the drama, the fears, or the awkward parts of leading people. In fact, it can exacerbate those very things.
3. If friendship at work increases engagement, productivity, enjoyment, and retention—it would be so for leaders too.

The alternative to them bonding more with the people on their team is for them to be emotionally distant from their team and pull away—less authenticity, less positive reinforcement, less reliability. Leadership, above all else, *is* relationship. We know that trust is the goal, that Vulnerability and honesty are part of the currency, and collaboration is where the magic resides; but none of that happens in a vacuum alone. Our leaders *have* to be connected to us.

It's to the benefit of our employees, teams, departments, and organizations that our leaders not just lean into healthy relationships but model them, practice them, and excel at them. And in so doing, they might end up feeling a little more connected to someone else more than they do to us. And that's okay, isn't it? We do that too. It's normal. It doesn't mean there's scarcity, that our career won't progress, or that we're not appreciated—that's just our fear whispering. Maybe, just maybe, we can each take a little more responsibility for checking our own fears and jealousies about who our boss is close to and instead try to hold gratitude that they are healthy enough to connect with others, focus on building the healthiest relationship we can with them, and trust that they can still be a good leader to us all.

A phenomenal example is Kimberly, whom I met when I was the keynote speaker at a women's leadership conference she was hosting for female insurance agency owners. It was clear she had the respect of the hundreds of women in the room. And in her introduction of me I saw glimpses of why they adored her. Flashing photos up on the screen of her with a group of friends, who had all worked for her at some point, she said to everyone in the audience, "This is what I want for you. We can't do this alone." I can attest it's far too few executives who hire a friendship expert to come speak to their leaders, but even fewer still who proudly talk about their own friendships developed from work and share the benefits they've experienced. Kimberly gets together with her eight former employees for an annual girls' trip—they've been doing it for almost two decades. I've heard so many stories like this. Stories of emotionally intelligent humans forming friendships that extended beyond the lines of their roles.

In the next chapter I am going to teach how all of us can build healthier and more appropriate friendships at work; if you're a leader who values healthy relationships, it'll be your responsibility to model those behaviors—including the hard conversations.

And for the rest of us who find ourselves getting fearful about favoritism, let's take a deep breath and remember that our peace will come not from preventing or begrudging the connections of others but in examining our own feelings and doing the work to build the connections we want.

HOW TO RESPOND WHEN WE FEAR FAVORITISM

Very rarely are our bosses out there trying to make any one of us feel less than appreciated or valued. They may not be trained to be as competent or affirming as we wish they were, but the truth is that they really are doing the best they can with what they have right now. Most of them aren't waking up thinking, "How can I show preferential treatment to one person today and leave others feeling bad?" On the contrary, in fact, a recent study in the *Journal of Experimental Social Psychology* showed that supervisors are actually more prone to show a bias against their favorites in order to seem impartial.[3] (Which isn't what we want either, but it does show how much our supervisors are trying to be fair.)

But it doesn't always feel that way.

Roger resented his boss because she appeared so chummy with some of the other women at the loan processing division where they all worked. When I unpacked that with him, he realized that he actually had little desire to stand in her office talking with her like some of his colleagues did; but he was more afraid that by others doing it, his chances of being promoted would be impacted.

That's a big aha. It's powerful when we can start with identifying whether we're "jealous," which means we fear losing something or someone to someone else, or "envious," which means someone has something we desire. In Roger's shoes, some of us might identify that we're envious—we *want* to be closer to our boss. But in his case, he didn't so much want to be her friend as much as he felt jealous because he didn't want to lose out on a possible promotion. Starting with self-assessment helps us know the best path forward.

If he didn't realize that soon enough to do something about it, what probably would have affected his chances of being overlooked more than anything would have been that unchecked resentment showing up in passive-aggressive or sabotaging ways in the office. Instead, though, he ended up talking with her and sharing the growth he hoped to experience and asking her what she felt he could do that would best prepare him for that someday promotion. On that track, with her coaching him for growth, he realized he was less threatened by her social interactions.

We picked a favorite stuffed animal when we were toddlers, we have foods we love, and we will enjoy some people more than others. We all have certain people we feel closer to, trust in certain situations more, or feel will be a better fit for a certain project or task. Not only do we not leave our preferences at home when we come to work, that ability to choose one thing over another is what helps us

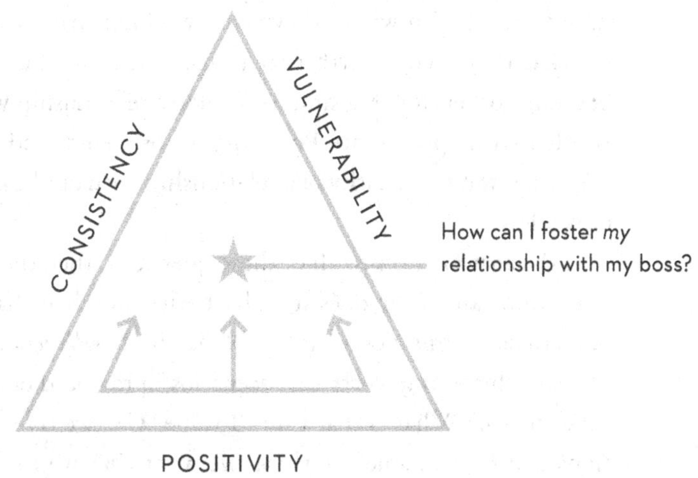

make decisions and do our jobs efficiently. It's not realistic, or even healthy, to expect those around us not to have "favorites."

The question here isn't so much whether our bosses have people they prefer or trust and rely upon as much as whether we've developed the healthiest relationship with them that we can.

- Have we been reliable?
- Do they know our strengths?
- Do they feel supported and encouraged by us?
- Have we asked them recently to share with us where they think we have the most room to grow?
- Have we practiced generosity with them—with credit, with praise, and with generous interpretations of their behaviors?
- Have we built trust by admitting when we don't know something?
- Would they have any reason to believe that we don't have their best interest at heart?

If the answer to any of those questions is no, then it probably isn't too hard to comprehend why they don't gravitate to us, prefer us, or feel safe with us. We have our work cut out to become someone they can trust and with whom they enjoy working. And if we protest and say that they aren't worth that to us, that's fine, but then we can't begrudge others for choosing to develop a relationship with them that is filled with appropriate Positivity, Consistency, and Vulnerability. We either want as healthy of a relationship with our bosses as possible, or we don't.

If the answer is yes to all of those questions, then the real questions to examine are: Why does it really bother me then that my boss appears to have some closer friends? What am I *really* feeling? Is this just my ego whispering worst-case scenarios in my head or is something I value at risk? What is that thing I value? Can we try on different options and try to name the thing we want that we think is missing?

More of their attention? Their friendship? A promotion? Assurance that my job is safe? More enjoyment in the workplace like they seem to experience? Clarity in what's expected of me? Understanding of how roles are distributed? The feeling of being special? More empathy for my situation? What specifically does that friendship represent to me that I think can either get me something I need or protect something I don't want to lose?

Allan, who was the lead on a product launch, shared with me how much he wished one of his employees had come to him earlier. "I had no idea how annoyed Kim was with Mike, but she felt I favored Mike's ideas, opinions, and suggestions over hers." Unfortunately, without her asking, "How can I help make sure my ideas are heard?" she unconsciously chose the route of undermining Mike by basically asking, "How can I make his ideas look bad?"

This happens more than most of us even realize. When we feel threatened, it's often easier to look for a target to blame than it is for us to look for a way to improve a relationship. Kim ended up losing trust with her boss, and the team, as she developed a reputation for being the one who always harshly judged the ideas of others. I asked Allan what he wished he knew sooner, to which he said, "I honestly wish she had come to me and just said, 'I'm having a hard time feeling like my ideas are being heard in our team meetings. I know they're not all good ideas, but I really do want to be a team player and contribute as much as possible.' Had she done that, I not only would have been impressed with her commitment to our work, but it would have helped me examine whether there were better ways I could run the meetings to make sure everyone felt safe. Clearly there was a growth opportunity for me that we missed, and now the whole team feels unsafe brainstorming."

So our supervisors might gravitate to a colleague who makes them laugh a lot, might enjoy the way another can talk about a favorite activity with them, might lean heavily on someone who they know they can rely on for follow-through, or might frequently want one person's wise counsel because they appreciate the way that person approaches situations. None of that takes anything away from who we are, what we can contribute, and how we can develop the best relationship possible with them.

I'm not saying that close friendships with leaders are appropriate in every work setting. So much depends on the culture of each company, the type of work we're doing together, the makeup of a team, the emotional health of the friends, and the skills of the leader. But because some of us will bond across the lines of our roles, whether we mean to or not (or not want to "break up" just because one of us gets promoted), let's take responsibility to have more conversations for how we can support friendships in ways that minimize the downsides and maximize the potential.

May we each find our own way to make our biggest contribution at work and build our own meaningful connections, all while trying to trust others to do the same.

12

Becoming Best Friends at Work

How to Develop Appropriate Friendships That Benefit the Team

"I wouldn't be able to survive the crazy if I didn't have Jennifer there," said Amalia, a physical therapist who works on a team with six others, including her best friend. "And believe me, there is so much crazy." I'll spare you the stories that ensued—mostly about their boss acting unethically, but also plenty of stories about their cranky and demanding patients—but it ended with her reiterating again how much her friendship made the job tolerable.

They have built a solid friendship: they both joined a roller derby team last year that practices together weekly, they frequently attend baseball games together with their husbands during the season, and they've done a couple trips to Las Vegas together. But it's not how they moved their friendship to Frientimacy that impresses me as much as what they've done in the workplace that bears telling.

She and Jennifer made a pact to try to raise the morale of the other therapists, hoping to help offset what otherwise felt like a toxic environment. From decorating an unused bulletin board with "Getting to Know Your Therapist" photos and fun facts for the patients to see to coordinating holiday potlucks with everyone on the team—they recycled the energy their friendship gave them and shared it with the others.

It's all too easy to find our "Jennifer" and cling to the friendship that is developing, but if we want to move a friendship up the Triangle, we'd be wise to practice how we can best protect it from the pressures of work and use it to raise the sense of connection in our entire workplace.

Be Generous with Intentional Positivity to Everyone Else.

Our first call to order, as illustrated so beautifully by Amalia's story, is to extend the Positivity we feel with each other to those around us.

Be the joy. The responsibility of those of us who are enjoying our friends at work is to recycle that joy to the rest of the team. Our friendship should be a gift to everyone around us—they should *want* to be around us. Because we are comfortable with one another and enjoy one another, we can help set a tone of gratitude, humor, and fun at our team meetings, parties, and desks. Our closeness should be felt as something that envelops others in it with us when we're at work, not something that feels exclusive.

Express affirmation. To offset the insecurities that others might project on our friendship, we must make sure that no one doubts that we see and appreciate everyone else. It's crucial for both people in the friendship to step up their game and be known as people who cheerlead and voice appreciation. To that end, we'll do all we can to never give anyone reason to worry that we are competing with them, trying to elbow our way in, speaking poorly of them, or sabotaging them. On the contrary, we hope that they feel nothing but love from us.

(Especially true if we're friends with the manager. The manager's success is based on the success of the team—so be someone the manager can trust to intentionally help build up the members of the team.)

Increase the Vulnerability to Talk about Our Relationship

Second, both of us are going to step up our Vulnerability—in this case by being willing to honestly have conversations that can help safeguard our relationship from various possible threats.

Proactively talk about our relationship. If we're mature enough to build these friendships, then we're mature enough to talk about them.

Toward the end of a conversation one day about what they didn't like at work, Jennifer asked Amalia, "What can we do to help make sure we don't get sucked into the vortex of pessimism?" It validated there was an "us" and elicited a conversation that set them on the path to fostering fun around them.

And it's always easier to do so *before* there's a reason to do so. In other words, don't wait until issues come up. Try to think through as many of them ahead of time as possible. We can easily say to each other, "Hey, I've been loving our friendship and to help protect it from all the stuff that can come up in a shared workplace, would you be willing to meet for drinks one night when we can talk through what would feel best to each of us?"

Some possible questions:

- How do you think others feel about our friendship? Is there anything we could do differently to help them feel better/less worried?
- What would be the worst-case scenario you could imagine? What, if anything, could we do to help prevent some of those things from ever happening? How would you want me to respond in that situation if, God forbid, we ever find ourselves in that worst-case scenario?

- What will be the hardest part of this working relationship for you?
- If one of us ever feels like we have to tell the other one something that might hurt our feelings—how would you want me to do that?
- What kind of scenarios tend to stress you out the most? And what signals do you give off that would help me see what you're feeling?
- What boundaries do we want to put in place to help safeguard our working relationship and our friendship?
- If you could ask anything of me, what would it be?
- I know you well, but if you were to come with a warning label—what would it be? What could you share with me that would help me better protect us?
- What do you most need from me while we're at work?
- What are some of the most supportive things I can do for you at work? What feels helpful?

Basically, we want to have as many conversations ahead of time so that we both feel more confident that we can rely on the relationship in meaningful ways and feel better equipped for having to handle situations as they arise. These conversations help set healthy expectations, reminding us that just because we're friends doesn't mean we won't have some challenges ahead.

Keep clarity and confidentiality in each role. This one doesn't need a ton of explaining, but we don't break our confidences, or boundaries—either at work or in the friendship.

Most successful friendships at work include boundaries about how we treat each other differently at work than we do outside of work. One supervisor shared with me that they call it out by pretending to take a hat off when they say, "Okay, now I'm taking my friend hat off and am saying this as a boss." Another clarified, "Some days my friend barely even says more than hello to me at work, and I'm completely okay with that as we're both clear that we care for each other, but we have different roles in this building." And as one cadet in the Marine Corps said to me, "What happens in the barracks at night has no bearing on whether I salute my superiors the next morning." We don't forget our separate roles . . . nor take it personally when we sometimes have to act differently in each setting.

Furthermore, we don't tell our friend details or private information about projects or people at work that isn't theirs to know. Obviously, the longer we've known each other, the more we're mutually sharing and the safer we feel in the friendship. It's unrealistic to think we won't be processing decisions and ideas with each other that may put us into some gray territory, but that's all the more reason to be clear ahead of time what details aren't appropriate or when we need to be vague.

And, on the flip side, we don't bring personal stuff we know about each other to work. For example, if we were at our friend's house over the weekend, that probably doesn't need to be mentioned during the Monday morning group share. We don't need to hide that we're friends, but we definitely don't need to keep it in everyone's face.

Lastly, look for ways to assure others that we aren't talking about them. When a colleague references something they assume we know because our friend told us, we'll be quick to say, "Oh, actually I didn't know that. We're very careful to not talk about anyone on the team." A few blatant lines like that over time helps build the team trust.

View your friendship as the place to practice tough things. So often we mistake friendship as the place where we should let each other off easily, look the other way, expect blind loyalty, hope for favors, or avoid hurting feelings. That's all backwards. The closer we are to each other, the safer we should feel to practice flexing the relational muscles that help us both become better people. Our closest friends are the ones who know us best (Vulnerability), love us most (Positivity), and are most committed to us (Consistency), so those are the best places for us to practice such things as:

- setting boundaries
- asking for what we need
- sharing how their actions left us feeling
- giving loving, but honest feedback
- receiving feedback with the best of assumptions
- praising them when jealous
- giving voice to the unspoken issue we're tempted to avoid
- disagreeing respectfully
- revealing our insecurities and doubts
- expressing pride for ourselves without downplaying our strengths
- negotiating for our preferences and needs

The list could go on, but the point is, if we can't practice doing these skills with our friends, then what chance do we ever have of feeling more comfortable doing these important actions with our vendors, our customers, and our other team members? Our relationships are where we grow so if we're willing to take on the joy of having fun together, then it's also our responsibility to take on the Vulnerability of growth that comes with deep friendship.

This means we don't make excuses for each other without asking some honest questions. Neither do we confuse loyalty for keeping someone in a role that isn't working out. And we practice giving and receiving feedback, honestly meaning it when we say, "Do you think I read that wrong?" rather than practicing the defensiveness we might put up with someone we aren't as sure has our best interests in mind. One of the best gifts we can give each other is the chance to role-play hard things that we each have to do in our positions.

The moral of the story: make sure our friendship is making us a better person, a better leader, a better contributor. Friendship isn't something to hide behind but rather something to expand us.

Spend More Time Together Outside of Work and Leave Work Time for Others (Consistency)

As time and attention become our most valuable commodities in our relationships, it's important that we invest them to meet the needs of our team and protect our friendship.

Focus mostly on others while at work: This isn't to say we can't connect while at work, but we want to be very clear that the last thing our colleagues want is to feel left out or concerned that the two of us act as a unit. We don't need to sit next to each other in team meetings, eat lunch together every day, or be seen sitting for long periods of time in each other's office. We'll purposely mix with others at work parties, check in with colleagues about their weekends, and extend help to those around us. We remember that friendship isn't an all-or-nothing game, so just because we've found one person we love being around doesn't mean we don't still invest heavily in those around us with our curiosity, authenticity, and kindness. These actions, from both of us, help protect our coworkers and contribute to a more positive workplace.

Spend time with your friend outside of work: As we become closer to someone at work, it becomes increasingly important that we spend more time with each other away from the workplace. Extending the invitation to connect at other times not only ensures that our bonding isn't as visible of a threat to the team and isn't on the company's time, but it's the best way we can protect our friendship too. If we want to remain friends after the job eventually ends for one of us, the chances to do that increase exponentially if we've already practiced spending time together away from the office. This will take our friendship to a whole new level, allowing us to see each other in different areas of our lives, giving us the space to talk more about new subjects, and hopefully eventually meeting other people who are important to each of us.

HOW TO NAVIGATE THE WORKPLACE WHEN WE'RE NOT GETTING ALONG

But what about when things inevitably go wrong?

The quote I chose to open my book *Frientimacy* was by Dr. Frank Andrews, who sagely said, "It seems impossible to love people who hurt and disappoint us, yet there are no other kinds of people."[1] It's a painful realization that it's impossible to be close to someone without also suffering from hurt feelings, unmet needs, and shattered expectations. And, yes, even our friends at work will annoy us, frustrate us, and leave us questioning their actions.

That doesn't mean it's an unhealthy friendship, or that our friend is selfish or toxic. In fact, depending on how we both respond to it, it can be the catalyst that leaves us feeling closer, safer, and more trusting of each other down the road. Think of close family members or romantic partners—we don't feel safe with them because they've loved us perfectly the whole time, we feel safe with them because we've gone through hard things and still love each other on the other side.

But how to get there?

The First Step: Prioritize the Work

First and foremost, let's remember we have two relationships in this one person: a friend and a colleague. And much the same way healthy parents continue to love and "coparent" their children even when they are fighting (even if what they are fighting about involves the kids), we will commit to "coworking" well together—no matter what. We don't want the "kids" to suffer by speaking badly of the other parent, trying to get them to pick sides, fighting in front of them, or sabotaging the efforts of the other to care well for them. Even if a couple gets divorced and brings that romantic relationship to an end, they can still choose to be positive, contributing, and healthy coparents. Think of our work as "the kids," and when we're in front of them, they are our priority, which also means the other parent they love is our priority too.

TWO RELATIONSHIPS

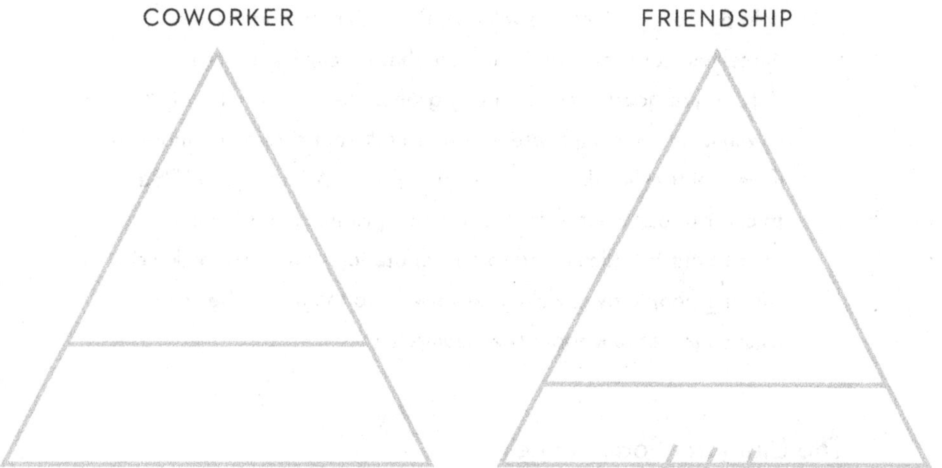

In a moment we'll look at how to reconcile as friends, but before that, and even if that never happens, let's be clear with each other that we are mature enough to work well together as colleagues. That could include:

- Writing a short email or note to our friend that says, "I just want you to know that even though I am still hurt/mad, you can be assured that while we're at work I will do everything possible to continue to support you." Clarifying our good intentions at work not only deescalates the situation for future reconnecting as friends, but it helps set the tone for both of us at work to be more thoughtful.
- Or having that conversation together: "I know we're both hurt right now and that we may not be quite ready to move on from this, but would you be willing to at least talk through what would feel best to both of us while we're at work? What can I do, or not do, to make sure this doesn't impact your job?"
- Choosing to blatantly support our friend at work to signal to them, and everyone else, who they can trust us to be during this

incident. Whether that's advocating one of their ideas during a team meeting, giving them credit in front of others, or offering to help on a big project—we will take the high road and prove to ourselves, our friend, and our team that we can be trusted.

- Refusing to gossip. It's so tempting when our egos are hurt to try to win over some supporters who can take our side—even more so if we feel they've already heard "the other side of the story." But to cater to our wounds in this situation just adds more wounds—both to our friendship and to our reputation. When we think we're winning people over, we're really saying to them that they can't trust us to not talk about them someday.

The Ultimate Goal: Peace

We don't have to know right now if we're going to make up, break up, or simply move the relationship down the Triangle a bit. What we do know is that we want to feel peace.

And the way there is through our Emotional Intelligence (EQ). At its simplest, EQ is the ability to:

1. accurately identify what we're feeling at any given time and
2. know what we need to do to manage that feeling and move us back to a place of peace.

Recognizing our emotions sounds easy enough, but the authors of *Emotional Intelligence 2.0* report that only 36 percent of people tested can correctly identify their emotions as they happen.[2] That means two out of three of us are walking around misnaming our emotions. Nearly all of us know how easy it can be to say we're *hungry* when we're actually *bored*, to say we're *threatened* when we're really *embarrassed*, or to say we're *annoyed* when we're simply *tired*.

I know, for me, when the stakes are high it can be hard to peel back the onion of emotions enough to honestly inquire, what am I *really, really, really* feeling? Often my first response, after being triggered, might be to claim I'm *mad* or *frustrated* as though anyone would feel the same way if their friend did X. But that'd just me being emotionally lazy. In my best moments, I can hopefully land more clearly: I feel *dismissed* because they didn't acknowledge how important that was to me, I feel *insecure* because I don't know if I can trust them to want my happiness, or I feel *let down* because I really wanted what they were offered. I may have manifested it with irritation, but what am I *really* feeling?

Most of us wish we had more clarity in our lives, and yet we routinely neglect the information constantly being dispatched. Emotions are our brain's way of sending us a message to pay attention to something that matters; any mistranslation risks us not receiving the intended message. Far too many of us are walking around ignoring, or blatantly dismissing, the very memos that our bodies are helpfully wired to deliver to us. What are we *really* feeling in this fight?

After we can name our emotions, we can then ask a few strategic questions, such as: What information does this emotion give me about myself and what I need? Is there anything I want to do with this information right now that might be productive or positive? What wisdom is available to me about how to best proceed?

This is the second step of EQ: taking responsibility for managing our actions in such a way that we can successfully return to contentment, or happiness, as soon as possible.

The more clarity we had in naming our emotions, the more a strategy for response becomes clear. For example:

- If we really felt *envy* (wanting something that someone else has) when our friend didn't invite us to lunch with another colleague but mistranslated it as *jealousy* (fear of losing something or someone to someone else)—we might be at risk of wanting to sabotage their relationship rather than admitting we wished we had been there as well. We now can respond in a way that increases our chances of being included next time as opposed to reacting in such a way that we lose them both.

- Or if we really felt *unappreciated* when our friend appeared to take all the credit on a project (or sale) but mistranslated that as feeling *betrayed*—we might be at risk of devaluing their legitimate contribution rather than inquiring what kind of recognition we need. We can now respond in a way that increases our chances of being seen as opposed to reacting in such a way that leaves our friend feeling unappreciated.
- Or if we really felt *angry* at them for crossing a boundary we said was important to us but mistranslated that as *disappointment*—we might be at risk of sulking and trying to get attention from others rather than confronting our friend to better clarify our needs and preferences. We can now respond in a way that increases our chances of healthy communication with our friend as opposed to reacting in passive-aggressive ways.

If we can take the time to self-reflect enough that we can identify what we're *really* feeling then we can better ask, "What response increases the odds of me returning to a place of peace as quickly as possible?"

The best path forward is always to try to repair the friendship—especially so if this is someone we've loved, cared for, or felt close to. We can try. The best-case scenario is that we learn more about each other through this miscommunication and feel closer on the other side. The worst-case scenario is we need to move the friendship down a notch or two on our Triangle (no matter how personally we took something, very rarely do the actions mean the other person needs to be dropped all the way down!). There we lower our expectations a bit, grieve the loss of what we thought we had, and feel proud that we strengthened our relational muscles by at least trying. We'll then remember that this is someone we still treat with kindness, clarity, and curiosity—staying open to what might heal and grow at future times.

Above all, we'll see two different relationship roles here—the colleague and the friend—and we'll clarify which relationship sustained the injury, so we can hopefully keep the other one as protected and safe as possible while we heal this one.

How to Protect Our Relationships from Unwanted Romantic Bonding

But just as some of us are afraid of fighting with a friend at work, some of us are also afraid of bonding too much with someone. There is perhaps no question with stronger opinions and more intense feelings than the topic of forming close friendships at work with the gender to whom we're attracted. With more than 50 percent of women and 44 percent of men admitting they have had a "work spouse"[3]—a bond with a coworker that resembles that of a married couple but is purely platonic—the friendships are clearly happening. But that's not to say we're comfortable with it, at all. Especially if we're the romantic partner of someone who has this close friendship. For just as the workplace is the number one place for friendships to start, it's also the number one place where affairs begin.[4] What makes it so hard, of course, is that the vast majority of affairs start off innocently with friendship as the only intention.

But as we now know, wherever there is Consistency, Positivity, and Vulnerability, so too will there be a bond. It's impossible to work on a team with those three things and not feel close to each other. But this is where the Triangle might, again, be helpful. Seeing the progression of levels reminds us that perhaps the answer to whether we can be friends with people of the gender to whom we're attracted is not so much a clear-cut yes or no across the board, as much as a "yes, but to an intentional degree." For every story we hear of someone having an affair they swore would never happen, we can also find a story of two people maintaining and enjoying what they swear is a meaningful and completely platonic friendship.

Which is good news as we hopefully can get even better at maintaining platonic friendships with boundaries as we move further away from heteronormative conditioning that sees each other only as romantic, or sexual, interests. We not only desperately need more healthy cross-gender friendships in the workplace as we are all striving toward more equality for women (which includes mentoring, socializing, and friendships with men), but we also recognize just how lonely it would be to someone who identifies as bisexual if we believed they couldn't be friends with anyone whom they might ever be attracted.

While this could be a whole book unto itself, here are a few guidelines I humbly offer:

1. **We strive for the highest level possible of intimacy in our romantic relationship.** Unfortunately, too many marriages and partnerships aren't great examples of high Positivity, high Vulnerability, and high Consistency. We fall into patterns in which we hide parts of ourselves out of shame, avoid sharing things to minimize conflict, are too busy to really spend time together in meaningful ways, or have neglected all the actions of Positivity that leave us feeling close, including affirmation, enjoyment, empathy, and laughter. First and foremost, if we want to protect our romantic relationship from other bonds, we start by keeping that relationship as high on the Triangle as we possibly can—which also means having honest and loving conversations about all our other relationships. If we catch ourselves hiding something from them, that might be a warning sign we're prioritizing another bond over this one.
2. **We remember that attraction is not the same as action, that bonds aren't all-or-nothing, and that we'll inevitably bond with many people in many different ways.** We're healthiest and happiest when we have a full Triangle holding as many meaningful relationships as we can foster. While it's a romantic notion that there's one person out there who is meant to be our *everything,* the truth is that all of us are nourished in different ways by different relationships. Building a bond with someone else doesn't mean we

don't love our life partner, that what we share isn't special, or that just because we have room in our heart for more connection means that other connections are at risk. We will bond with lots of people in our lives to a varying degree of intimacy. And none of us are victims to how much we bond with someone—that is the result of the actions we take.

3. **We ask the bigger question: To what degree are we comfortable bonding outside of a committed romantic relationship?** This is a question all people will have to answer for themselves . . . hopefully with input from their romantic partner. For example, if we feel that the third level, familiarity, is as high up as we want a specific relationship to grow, then we want to be thoughtful to list what self-appointed boundaries feel best for containing the bond. In other words, if what moves people into the fourth level, commitment, are things like spending time outside of work, relying on each other for nonwork support, processing and asking advice about our personal relationships, or expressing our mutual adoration—we would be wise to clearly protect that line before we reach it.

One of my friends, Greg, whose best friend is a woman he used to teach with, has a rule called "Firsts and Bests"

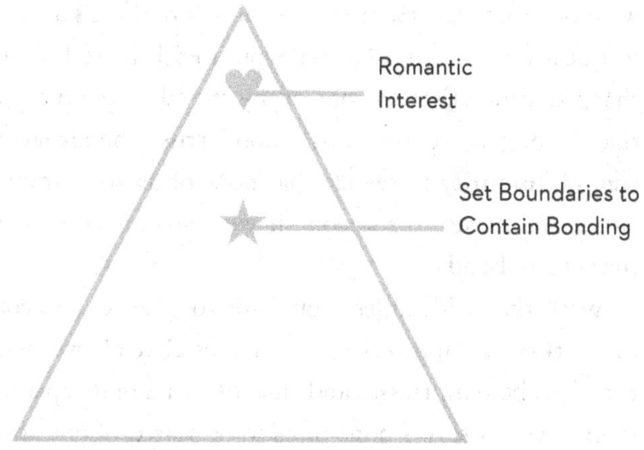

with his wife. Essentially, he not only makes sure she gets to hear things about his life from him first and gets the best of him, but it also means she gets first dibs on whether she wants to join him for a specific event; and she knows that certain actions (like buying flowers, in their case) is a gift reserved for her.

In a primarily male-dominated tech company, Amy and her fiancé have talked through a couple of strategies to help her strengthen her friendships in her field. Her fiancé joins her and her colleagues, as much as possible, for after-work drinks and rounds of pool with the stated purpose of "being her wingman" to help her have the chance to socialize and connect. In addition, they both agree that if there's a coworker she ever feels some attraction to, she'd do everything she could not to spend alone time with him until the attraction passes. Their attraction-at-times-assumed approach normalizes that it will happen with hopes that admitting it can minimize shame and jealousy.

As there are so many different expressions of marriage, such varying degrees of personal maturity, and such distinct aspects of what would feel important to each of us, it's impossible to give a clear list that would work for everyone. I always advise having a conversation with our romantic partners—even before there's a specific friendship in question—about what we would each hope for, and need, when that situation arises. As one of my friends is good at saying, "It's not that I don't trust him, but I don't trust the situation." Let's hold enough humility to realize that none of us are immune from feeling closer and closer to someone if we continue to practice the actions that create bonds.

With that said, unless you want to believe, and continue to reinforce, the disempowering caricatures that all women are out there trying to be temptresses and that all men are incapable of controlling themselves, it serves none of us to be scared of one another and make rules based on worst-case scenarios and fears. I'd love to believe, assuming I feel safe, that there isn't anyone with whom I couldn't ride an elevator, share a meal, or mentor. I obviously will listen to my intuition each time, but, in general, I will assume the best of others and trust my own wisdom.

WE ABSOLUTELY CAN DEVELOP HEALTHY BEST FRIENDS AT WORK

The details vary, but the support we feel from combining two of the most significant parts of our lives—our belonging and our work—can't be minimized. There are millions of stories like Jennifer and Amalia. And if you want a closer friendship in your life that starts at your workplace, then I want it for you. Just remember, the three most important actions we can take as we deepen our own friendships at work are:

1. **Positivity:** Be extra intentional *about expressing appreciation and kindness* to everyone else around us.

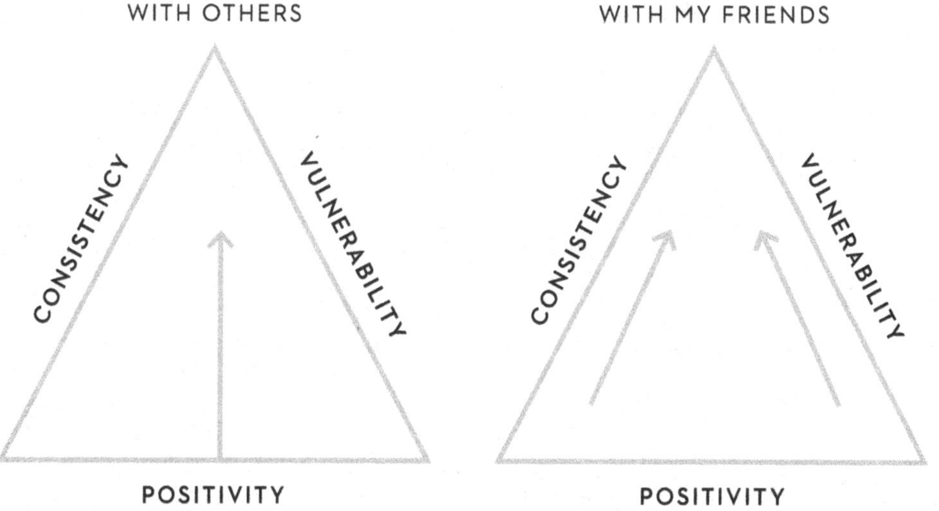

2. **Vulnerability:** Increase our honesty to talk about our relationship and practice the hard things.
3. **Consistency:** Practice new ways of spending time together outside of work and leave work time for others as much as possible.

Hopefully more of us see the responsibility that comes with relationship. These connections, to be both meaningful and appropriate, aren't just where we get to vent and get our own needs cared for, but they are also where we practice the skills that make us better people.

In Closing

After looking at all the things that could go wrong, it's easy to see why so many of us might just shake our heads and say, "Not worth it." But allow me a final moment as I briefly summarize how it's in the building of our relationships, not the avoiding of them, that we improve all other areas of our lives and our world.

Some of you may think I'm naïve to state that "friendships can change the world." But I believe it to my core. When we become more practiced at the competencies of friendship with the people around us, we are then better equipped to respond to every crisis, dilemma, or problem in our personal world and in our bigger shared world. Our solutions for pretty much everything big—including poverty, terrorism, war, sexism, racism, sex slavery, immigration, political breakdown, and religious injustices—are rooted in our ability to become less defensive, less selfish, less territorial, and more collaborative, more empathetic, and more emotionally intelligent. Those skills and outcomes are practiced only in our relationships with others.

We can go to a workshop on diversity, but we have to be in relationship with someone different from us before we get the benefit of having our world expanded; we can read a book on better leadership, but we have to be in relationship with someone to actually practice leading them; we can watch a convincing TED Talk on increasing our Vulnerability, but we have to be in relationship with someone to practice sharing more of ourselves in appropriate and meaningful ways. Personal growth might be sparked in our solitude, but the growth never happens without us bumping up against each other as we figure out how to be in relationship with others. We don't become our best selves outside of relationships.

The skills we get to practice with the people in our work are the same skills that will lead us to greater peace and happiness in all other areas of our lives and will be of the greatest service to the biggest challenges in our world. Every problem comes down to people needing to learn to work together. We might as well start with the people in our corner of the workplace.

The truth is that we either believe the research that we perform better, and are happier, when we feel like we belong . . . or we don't.

It's time for us to either:

1. **admit we don't believe all the studies,** research, and feedback from millions of people showing the positive impact that friendship has in the workplace, an admission that results in us choosing to keep expressing our negative opinion as though it's more informed and can counteract the mountains of data; or
2. **start looking for brave ways to start practicing new ways of fostering friendship at work.** We can still acknowledge that we're a bit scared about what it looks like or how to do it—as few of us have had it modeled to us well—but we'll at least stop resisting, or ignoring, the data and start looking for more solutions.

In general, there really is little we can do that will positively affect our lives more than fostering friendships wherever we are; but more specifically, if we can do it at work then we powerfully enhance the effect in our lives as we watch our health, happiness, and job satisfaction all boost one another.

I invite you to be one more advocate in this world who uses your influence, your platform, and your voice to encourage healthy friendships. We have important work to do in this world. We might as well enjoy doing it together as much as we possibly can. #thebusinessoffriendship

About Free Bonus Chapter

With work being the number one place where most of us are making our best friends, it comes as a painful surprise to most of us that it's also the place where most friendships end. And not because the majority of those friendships blew up or disappointed us but rather because of something far more innocent: one of us changed jobs.

Get your free bonus chapter, "Keeping the Friendship after the Job: How to Transition Our Friendships When We No Longer Work Together," at www.thebusinessoffriendship.com.

Advice for Managers

We've all heard the gut-wrenching numbers of how low employee engagement is around the world, and how pretty much everything we want to accomplish—whether it's productivity, creativity, or stellar customer service—hinges on that one statistic. But what we often forget is that their engagement has 70 percent more to do with the way they are managed than any other single factor. As Dr. Jim Harter, the chief scientist for Workplace and Wellbeing at Gallup, says, "Performance fluctuates widely and unnecessarily in most companies, in no small part from the lack of Consistency in how people are managed."[1] Your role is nothing short of powerful, to say the least!

You accepted the position of being responsible for the morale, productivity, vision-casting, and motivation on your team, and since your team is made up of individuals who all accomplish those things with different strengths, who feel appreciated in different ways, and who each show up with different needs that need to be addressed, your task is to *see* each person on your team in a way that feels *safe* and *satisfying* to everyone who reports to you. Basically, leadership is relationship.

To that point, the most effective leadership style in most cases is no longer that of the stereotypical "taskmaster" who uses fear and micromanaging to get things done. Rather it's that of the "coach" who uses "the quality and quantity of their interactions with team members" to develop an "individualized understanding of each team member" with discussions mostly "strengths-based" for the purpose of coaching them "to be their best."[2] Those quotes come from Gallup's *The Real Future of Work* series, which are built from global data of effective leadership. But hopefully now we're attuned at identifying our Three Relationship Requirements in their definition. Our interaction with our direct reports needs to be frequent and regular (Consistency), for the purpose of us seeing each other's strengths and needs (Vulnerability), and based on us feeling appreciated and supported to be our best (Positivity).

Nearly 60 percent of us have left a job because of our direct supervisor. And even if we give reasons like wanting more money, the majority of us admit that we'd stay for a lower salary if we worked with a "great boss."[3] Further, if you add in the other top reasons people leave—unhealthy office politics, feeling undervalued, or feeling disrespected by our colleagues—we quickly have yet another reminder of just how crucial healthy and positive relationships at work are to those on our team.

If I were to sum up the three biggest actions I think more managers could do immediately to improve the relationships around them, these are the ones I'd pick:

1. **Err on the side of fostering the highest Positivity ratio you can.** There will be stress, disappointments, critical feedback, and unmet expectations whether we like it or not. But we can always focus on offsetting that as much as possible by remembering that Positivity—our team feeling good about themselves in our presence—is the foundation of our leadership. If we make it our goal to be a catalyst for positive emotions, then we are not only banking them for when we need to make withdrawals, but we're also modeling to them the behaviors we hope they practice with each other. Ask yourself:

    - Do I know my employees' strengths well enough that I can watch for them using it and express appreciation in real time?

- Is there an easy way I can facilitate more consistent cheering, celebrating, or appreciation in our workplace?
- What's a positive emotion that matters to me (for example, gratitude, fun, empathy, amusement, hope) and what actions would help me authentically feel more of that in my job?
- Going down the list of my employees, using a scale of 1–10, how positive does each relationship feel? Of the lowest ones, what might I experiment with to try to purposely raise those scores?

2. **Initiate conversations and assessments that lead to more team-initiated solutions.** In line with our role as coaches, it's not our job to have all the answers as much as it is to provide the space for us to ask the right questions. I'm often brought in to facilitate the *Healthy Team Relationship Assessment* in order to give all team members the chance to score their experience on the team and calculate an overall team score in each of the Three Requirements. I've never followed it up with "so here's what you need to do to bring that score up." Rather, I say, "So let's break into small groups and brainstorm all the ways your team might increase that score." And to this day, there has never been a team that hasn't produced an entire list of creative ideas that are customized to that particular industry and team. Our job as coaches isn't to know *exactly* what we need to do to increase Consistency, Positivity, and Vulnerability on our teams as much as it's to broach the conversations that allow our team members to give honest feedback in a safe way and to value their ideas and suggestions.

   To that point, it can actually be to our detriment to think we have all the answers. In the above assessment, 80 percent of managers rate the health of their team relationships higher than their team members do. On average, managers tend to score their experience on a team ten points higher than the members of their team do; so we'd be wise to hold enough humility to realize that our experiences aren't usually the same as those on our team.

We can occasionally take the time to ask some of the following questions that can help foster more awareness and trust:

- What would help us all feel safer on this team when it comes to brainstorming?
- Let's go around the circle and each share what a reliable source of inspiration is for each of us. What tends to provoke our ideas, stimulate our thoughts, lift our spirits, or foster more hope?
- If we could be completely honest about how we would want someone to approach us if we were frustrating them, what advice would we give?
- Let's spend some time this morning talking about what the most meaningful way to celebrate the upcoming holiday together would be? Is it a party or something else? Let's throw all the ideas up on the board and vote on our favorites.
- Let's go around and give ourselves credit for something we did that no one else patted us on the back for this last week, or maybe even saw that we did it. I'll go first. "I pat myself on the back for doing . . ."
- Since communication is the bedrock of everything we do together, let's lay down some ground rules that leave us feeling like we can better rely on each other. You make suggestions of what would feel important and I'll list them on the board up here.

3. **Be vocal that you want your team to have healthy friendships and provide the training and time for them to foster them in healthy ways.** When asked if "My manager/boss intentionally fosters friendships on the team," only 13 percent of respondents on the *Friendships in the Workplace Survey* said, "definitely true."

My manager/boss intentionally fosters friendships on the team				
Definitely True	*Probably True*	*I Don't Know*	*Probably False*	*Definitely False*
13%	25%	19%	19%	24%

Even if we add those who claim it's "probably true," that still means only about a third of our workforce feels that they can credit us with attempting to foster healthy friendships.

We can, at minimum, frequently repeat how important it is to us that they foster healthy friendships here at work. Then, we can begin to look for ways to:

- Share the data with them on how much workplace friendships impact our productivity and engagement, so they know they have our permission and encouragement to foster friendships.
- Bring in trainers, speakers, and facilitators who can help us inspire and train our team to foster healthy expectations, answer questions, and help our team role-play scenarios that will give them better overall people skills. We can continue to embed it in our culture by ongoing workshops or lunch-and-learns that focus on specific aspects such as the power of empathy at work, how to minimize gossip at work, and healthy conflict management.

- Plan off-site meetings that have protected time away from the office for our teams to have fun together and make memories.
- Work with our department or larger organization to possibly make this the focus of a campaign or initiative. The organization where my sister works (44,000 employees worldwide) stated their annual goal "to raise the number of employees who have a best friend at work" and then regularly sent out ideas in newsletters, fostered events for meeting new friends, and ran contests giving away free lunches for employees who snapped photos of themselves with a workplace friend.

The outcome of building strong relationships with each employee is that they feel more loyal (an outcome of Consistency), more appreciated (an outcome of Positivity), and more valued for who they are (an outcome of Vulnerability).

May leaders like you rise up and change the way our workplaces feel about friendships. May you be an advocate who knows just how much it matters to have your team excited to show up at work and feel like they belong. May you be someone who isn't scared of the risks as much as you're motivated by the possibilities. And, may you foster the friendships in your own life that leave you feeling so very *seen* for all that you do and for who you are; so very *satisfied* and happy; and so very *safe* as you live with the peace of knowing you are completely supported.

Resources and Ideas for Friendships at Work

If we decrease loneliness in our workplaces, then we are essentially impacting the way we do health care, education, religion, politics, and technology. My hope for this book has always been more than me putting words on pages but rather that in reading this book we give ourselves permission to foster the friendships that will leave this world a better place. Below are some ideas and tools to take this from a book and into our lives:

#TheBusinessofFriendship Join the conversation, share your tips and stories, and encourage those around you to foster the friendships that will benefit their lives and their workplaces. And post a photo with your business friend adding **#BizBuddies** to affirm them and inspire others! (And I'm @ShastaMNeslon.)

Host a Book Club I've written two different book guides—one is for the traditional "meet once and discuss the book" format, and the other is a "let's meet four times and discuss the book while we build up our own friendships with each other" format. Both are available at www.thebusinessoffriendship.com.

Download a Worksheet There are several extra resources for you and your team at www.thebusinessoffriendship.com.

Book Shasta Nelson to keynote your next conference, train your employees on healthy friendships, facilitate an off-site meeting for your team, or consult with your organization on how to change culture. For more information and to contact her agent, go to: https://www.shastanelson.com/speaking.

Shasta Nelson is a leading expert on friendship and healthy relationships, creator of a global community, keynote speaker, author of several books, and popular media resource. www.ShastaNelson.com.

Notes

Introduction

1. Shasta Nelson, "Friendships in the Workplace Survey," April 2019.
2. Cigna, "Loneliness and The Workplace 2020 U.S. Report," Cigna Health Corporation, 2020. Accessed at https://www.cigna.com/static/www-cigna-com/docs/about-us/newsroom/studies-and-reports/combatting-loneliness/cigna-2020-loneliness-report.pdf.
3. Annie McKee, *How to Be Happy at Work: The Power of Purpose, Hope and Friendships* (Boston: Harvard Business Review Press, 2018).
4. Aaron Hurst and Nicole Resch, "Pathways to Fulfillment at Work: The 2019 Workforce Purpose Index," Imperative, March 2019. Accessed at https://static1.squarespace.com/static/55f3a1b7e4b0d34cd55076ac/t/5ce20b787c744f0001932bfe/1558318088657/Imperative+2019+Workforce+Purpose+Index-eccoh+APAC.pdf.
5. Emma Seppälä and Marissa King, "Burnout at Work Isn't Just about Exhaustion. It's Also about Loneliness," *Harvard Business Review*, June 29, 2017. Accessed at https://hbr.org/2017/06/burnout-at-work-isnt-just-about-exhaustion-its-also-about-loneliness.
6. "Item 10: I Have a Best Friend at Work," Workplace, Gallup, Inc., May 26, 1999. Accessed at https://www.gallup.com/workplace/237530/item-best-friend-work.aspx.
7. Ira Glass, *This American Life*, July 19, 2018. Accessed at https://www.thisamericanlife.org/389/transcript.

Chapter 1

1. John T. Cacioppo and William Patrick, *Loneliness: Human Nature and the Need for Social Connection* (New York: W.W. Norton & Company, 2009).
2. "Cigna 2018 U.S. Loneliness Index," Cigna Health Corporation, 2018. Accessed at https://www.cigna.com/assets/docs/newsroom/loneliness-survey-2018-fact-sheet.pdf.
3. "Loneliness and The Workplace: 2020 U.S. Report," Cigna Health Corporation, 2020. Accessed at https://www.cigna.com/static/www-cigna-com/docs/about-us/newsroom/studies-and-reports/combatting-loneliness/cigna-2020-loneliness-report.pdf.

4. Hurst and Resch, "Pathways to Fulfillment at Work: The 2019 Workforce Purpose Index."
5. "Loneliness Causing UK Workers to Quit Their Jobs," Totaljobs.com Press Centre, Totaljobs Group Ltd, July 26, 2018. Accessed at http://press.totaljobs.com/release/loneliness-causing-uk-workers-to-quit-their-jobs/.
6. John Hilton, "Do Your Employees Feel Lonely at Work?" HRD Australia, July 8, 2019. Accessed at https://www.hcamag.com/au/specialisation/mental-health/do-your-employees-feel-lonely-at-work/172016.
7. "Loneliness and The Workplace 2020 U.S. Report."
8. Hannah Ewens, "What Young People Fear the Most," Vice, September 21, 2016. Accessed at https://www.vice.com/en_uk/article/nnyk37/what-vice-readers-fear-the-most-hannah-ewens-love-loneliness.
9. "State of Women's Wellness 2017," Everyday Health, 2017. Accessed at https://images.agoramedia.com/everydayhealth/gcms/Everyday-Health-State-of-Womens-Wellness-Survey-PDF.pdf.
10. Vivek Murthy, "Work and the Loneliness Epidemic," *Harvard Business Review*, September 26, 2017. Accessed at https://hbr.org/cover-story/2017/09/work-and-the-loneliness-epidemic.
11. Nicole K. Valtorta, Mona K. Kanaan, Simon K. Gilbody, Barbara K. Hanratty, and Sara K. Ronzi, "Loneliness and Social Isolation as Risk Factors for Coronary Heart Disease and Stroke: Systematic Review and Meta-Analysis of Longitudinal Observational Studies," *Heart Volume* 102, Issue 13 (June 10, 2016). Accessed at https://heart.bmj.com/content/102/13/1009.
12. Julianne B. Holt-Lunstad, Timothy B. Smith, and J. Bradley B. Layton, "Social Relationships and Mortality Risk: A Meta-Analytic Review," *PLOS Medicine* (July 27, 2010). Accessed at https://doi.org/10.1371/journal.pmed.1000316.
13. Dean Ornish, *Love and Survival: 8 Pathways to Intimacy and Health* (New York: Collins Living, 1999).
14. L. Berkman and L. Breslow, *Health and Ways of Living: The Alameda County Study* (New York: Oxford University Press, 1983).
15. Simone Schnall, Kent D. Harber, Jeanine K. Stefanucci, and Dennis R. Proffitt, "Social Support and the Perception of Geographical Slant," PMC, National Center for Biotechnology Information, September 1, 2008. Accessed at https://www.ncbi.nlm.nih.gov/pmc/articles/PMC3291107/.
16. Ilan Mochari, "One Surprising Way to Boost Workplace Productivity," Why Having a BFF at Work Matters More Than You Think," *Inc.*, April 18, 2016. Accessed at https://www.inc.com/ilan-mochari/best-friend-at-work-oc-tanner-survey.html.
17. James A. Coan, Hillary S. Schaefer, and Richard J. Davidson, "Lending a Hand: Social Regulation of the Neural Response to Threat," *Psychological Science* 17, Issue 12 (December 2006), pp. 1032–1039. Accessed at https://doi.org/10.1111/j.1467-9280.2006.01832.x.
18. Shasta Nelson, "Your Brain on Friendships," GirlFriendCircles.com, March 19, 2013. Accessed at https://www.girlfriendcircles.com/blog/index.php/2013/03/your-brain-on-friendships.
19. Ning Xia and Huige Li, "Loneliness, Social Isolation, and Cardiovascular Health," *Antioxidants & Redox Signaling* 28, no. 9 (March 20, 2018), pp. 837–851. Accessed at https://www.ncbi.nlm.nih.gov/pmc/articles/PMC5831910/.
20. William Ruberman, Eve Weinblatt, Judith D. Goldberg, and Banvir S. Chaudhary, "Psychosocial Influences on Mortality After Myocardial Infarction,"

New England Journal of Medicine 311, no. 9 (August 30, 1984), pp. 552–559. Accessed at https://www.nejm.org/doi/full/10.1056/NEJM198408303110902.

21. Tara Parker-Pope, "What Are Friends For? A Longer Life." *New York Times*, April 20, 2009. Accessed at https://www.nytimes.com/2009/04/21/health/21well.html.
22. Sheldon Cohen, William J. Doyle, David P. Skoner, et al, "Social Ties and Susceptibility to the Common Cold," *Journal of the American Medical Association* 277, no. 24 (June 25, 1997), pp. 1940–1944. Accessed at doi:10.1001/jama.1997.03540480040036.
23. "Fall 2014 Report: The Effect of Work Relationships on Organizational Culture and Commitment." Workforce Mood Tracker, Globoforce Limited, 2014. Accessed at http://go.globoforce.com/rs/globoforce/images/Fall_2014_Mood_Tracker.pdf.
24. David Niven, *The 100 Simple Secrets of Happy People: What Scientists Have Learned and How You Can Use It* (New York: HarperCollins e-books, 2009).
25. Robert D. Putnam, *Bowling Alone: The Collapse and Revival of American Community* (New York: Simon & Schuster, 2007).
26. Bianca DiJulio, Liz Hamel, Cailey Muñana, and Mollyann Brodie, "Loneliness and Social Isolation in the United States, the United Kingdom, and Japan: An International Survey," Kaiser Family Foundation, August 2018. Accessed at https://www.kff.org/other/press-release/survey-one-in-five-americans-report-loneliness-social-isolation/.
27. Tom Rath and James K. Harter, *Wellbeing: The Five Essential Elements* (New York: Gallup Press, 2014).
28. Rath and Harter, *Wellbeing: The Five Essential Elements*.

Chapter 2

1. "Relationships with Coworkers Matter Most for Well-Being at Work, Research Suggest," Cision PR Newswire, May 29, 2019. Accessed at https://www.prnewswire.com/news-releases/relationships-with-coworkers-matter-most-for-well-being-at-work-research-suggest-300858494.html.
2. John Hilton, "Do Your Employees Feel Lonely at Work?"
3. "The Cost of Loneliness to UK Employers," New Economics Foundation, March 7, 2019. Accessed at https://neweconomics.org/2017/02/cost-loneliness-uk-employers/.
4. "Fall 2014 Report: The Effect of Work Relationships on Organizational Culture and Commitment."
5. Jake Herway, "How to Bring Out the Best in Your People and Your Company," Gallup Workplace, March 6, 2018. Accessed at https://www.gallup.com/workplace/232958/bring-best-people-company.aspx.
6. "Item 10: I Have a Best Friend at Work," Workplace, Gallup, Inc., August 21, 2019. Accessed at https://www.gallup.com/workplace/237530/item-best-friend-work.aspx.
7. Jessica Bird, "Pay Is Not the Main Driver of Job Satisfaction, Shows Study from Indeed," Employee Benefits, May 10, 2018. Accessed at https://www.employeebenefits.co.uk/53-employees-not-think-paid-appropriately/.
8. "Bringing More Humanity to Recognition, Performance, and Life at Work," Workhuman Research Institute, May 2017. Accessed at https://www.workhuman.com/resources/research-reports/bringing-more-humanity-to-recognition-performance-and-life-at-work?

9. Paul Petrone, "How to Calculate the Cost of Employee Disengagement," LinkedIn Learning, March 24, 2017. Accessed at https://learning.linkedin.com/blog/engaging-your-workforce/how-to-calculate-the-cost-of-employee-disengagement.
10. "Loneliness Causing UK Workers To Quit Their Jobs."
11. Amy Edmondson, "Psychological Safety and Learning Behavior in Work Teams," *Administrative Science Quarterly* 44, no. 2 (June 1999), pp. 350–383. Accessed at http://web.mit.edu/curhan/www/docs/Articles/15341_Readings/Group_Performance/Edmondson Psychological safety.pdf.
12. Edmondson, "Psychological Safety and Learning Behavior in Work Teams."
13. "The State of American Jobs," Pew Research Center's Social & Demographic Trends Project, Pew Research Center, October 9, 2017. Accessed at https://www.pewsocialtrends.org/2016/10/06/the-state-of-american-jobs/.
14. Alain Elkann, "Minouche Shafik." Alain Elkann Interviews, June 7, 2018. Accessed at https://www.alainelkanninterviews.com/minouche-shafik/.
15. "The State of American Jobs," Pew Research Center, October 9, 2017.
16. "Loneliness Causing UK Workers To Quit Their Jobs."

Chapter 3

1. Mady W. Segal, "Alphabet and Attraction: An Unobtrusive Measure of the Effect of Propinquity in a Field Setting," *Journal of Personality and Social Psychology* 30, no. 5 (1974), pp. 654–657. Accessed at https://psycnet.apa.org/record/1975-07300-001.
2. Arthur Aron, Edward Melinat, Elaine N. Aron, Robert Darrin Vallone, and Renee J. Bator, "The Experimental Generation of Interpersonal Closeness: A Procedure and Some Preliminary Findings," *Personality and Social Psychology Bulletin* 23, no. 4 (April 1997), pp. 363–377. Accessed at doi: 10.1177/0146167297234003.
3. Charles Duhigg, "What Google Learned from Its Quest to Build the Perfect Team," *New York Times Magazine*, February 25, 2016. Accessed at https://www.nytimes.com/2016/02/28/magazine/what-google-learned-from-its-quest-to-build-the-perfect-team.html.
4. Julie Beck, "How Friendships Change When You Become an Adult," the *Atlantic*, October 26, 2015. Accessed at https://www.theatlantic.com/health/archive/2015/10/how-friendships-change-over-time-in-adulthood/411466/.
5. Debra L. Oswald, Eddie M. Clark, and Cheryl M. Kelly, "Friendship Maintenance: An Analysis of Individual and Dyad Behaviors," *Journal of Social and Clinical Psychology* 23, no. 3 (2004), pp. 413–441. Accessed at https://doi.org/10.1521/jscp.23.3.413.35460.
6. Edmondson, "Psychological Safety and Learning Behavior in Work Teams."
7. William A. Kahn, "Psychological Conditions of Personal Engagement and Disengagement at Work," *Academy of Management Journal* 33, no. 4 (December 1, 1990). Accessed at https://doi.org/10.5465/256287.

Chapter 5

1. "2019 Jobs Rated Report on Stress." CareerCast.com, March 6, 2019. Accessed at https://www.careercast.com/jobs-rated/2019-jobs-rated-stress.
2. Tom W. Smith, "General Social Survey, 2016," The Association of Religion Data Archives, 2016. Accessed at http://www.thearda.com/Archive/Files/Descriptions/GSS2016.asp.

3. Aimee Picchi, "Crying on the Job? You're Not Alone, with 8 in 10 Workers Shedding Tears," CBS News, August 15, 2019. Accessed at https://www.cbsnews.com/news/crying-on-the-job-youre-not-alone-with-8-in-10-workers-shedding-tears/.
4. "Survey: 64% of Americans Have Nightmares about Work," SleepZoo, May 29, 2018. Accessed at https://sleepzoo.com/nightmares-about-work/.
5. Danielle Boyd, "Workplace Stress," The American Institute of Stress, March 28, 2019. Accessed at https://www.stress.org/workplace-stress.
6. Boyd, "Workplace Stress."
7. Amy J. C. Cuddy, Susan T. Fiske, and Peter Glick, "Warmth and Competence as Universal Dimensions of Social Perception: The Stereotype Content Model and the BIAS Map," *Advances in Experimental Social Psychology* 40 (March 18, 2008), pp. 61–149. Accessed at https://www.sciencedirect.com/science/article/pii/S0065260107000020.
8. Barbara L. Fredrickson, *Positivity* (New York: Three Rivers Press, 2009).
9. Maria Ross, *Empathy Edge: Harnessing the Value of Compassion as an Engine for Success* (Page Two, 2019).
10. Stuart Hearn, "Your Employees Feel Underappreciated. Here's What You Can Do to Fix It," Business.com, June 28, 2017. Accessed at https://www.business.com/articles/stuart-hearn-improving-employee-performance-through-recognition/.
11. "Fall 2014 Report: The Effect of Work Relationships on Organizational Culture and Commitment," Workforce Mood Tracker. Globoforce Limited, 2014. Accessed at http://go.globoforce.com/rs/globoforce/images/Fall_2014_Mood_Tracker.pdf.
12. Maren Hogan, "5 Employee Feedback Stats That You Need to See," *LinkedIn Talent Blog*, February 8, 2016. Accessed at https://business.linkedin.com/talent-solutions/blog/trends-and-research/2016/5-Employee-Feedback-Stats-That-You-Need-to-See.
13. Ericka L. Rosenberg, Paul Ekman, Wei Jiang, Michael Babyak, R. Edward Coleman, Michael Hanson, Christopher O'Connor, Robert Waugh, and James A. Blumenthal, "Linkages between Facial Expressions of Anger and Transient Myocardial Ischemia in Men with Coronary Artery Disease," *Emotion* 1, no. 2 (June 2001), pp. 107–115. Accessed at https://www.researchgate.net/publication/6414393_Linkages_Between_Facial_Expressions_of_Anger_and_Transient_Myocardial_Ischemia_in_Men_With_Coronary_Artery_Disease.
14. Laura Delizonna, "High-Performing Teams Need Psychological Safety. Here's How to Create It," *Harvard Business Review*, August 24, 2017. Accessed at https://hbr.org/2017/08/high-performing-teams-need-psychological-safety-heres-how-to-create-it.

Chapter 6

1. Robert Kraut, Carmen Egido, and Jolene Galegher, "Patterns of Contact and Communication in Scientific Research Collaboration," *CSCW '88: Proceedings of the 1988 ACM Conference on Computer-Supported Academic Work,* January 1988, pp. 1–12. Accessed at https://doi.org/10.1145/62266.62267.
2. Ben Waber, "Technology for Workplaces That Work: Humanyze's Ben Waber," *MIT Technology Review*, January 24, 2019. Accessed at https://www.technologyreview.com/s/612814/technology-for-workplaces-that-work-humanyzes-ben-waber/.
3. "Should You Work from Home or at the Office? Science Has the Answer," Ladders, June 18, 2019. Accessed at https://www.theladders.com/career-advice/should-you-work-from-home-or-at-the-office-science-has-the-answer.

4. Glen H. Elder, and Elizabeth C. Clipp. "Wartime Losses and Social Bonding: Influences across 40 Years in Men's Lives," *Psychiatry* 51, no. 2 (May 1988), pp. 177–198. Accessed at https://doi.org/10.1080/00332747.1988.11024391.
5. Allison Master, Lucas P. Butler, and Gregory M. Walton, *Science of Interest* (Springer International Publishing, 2017).
6. Annie Dillard, *The Writing Life* (Harper Perennial, 2013).
7. Jim Harter, and Raksha Arora. "Social Time Crucial to Daily Emotional Well-Being in U.S." Gallup, Inc., June 5, 2008. Accessed at https://news.gallup.com/poll/107692/social-time-crucial-daily-emotional-wellbeing.aspx.
8. Mark Murphy, "What Do Great Leaders Discuss with Their Employees?" *Entrepreneur*, July 3, 2014. Accessed at https://www.entrepreneur.com/article/235298.
9. Tsedal Neeley and Paul Leonardi, "Defend Your Research: Effective Managers Say the Same Thing Twice (or More)," *Harvard Business Review*, June 8, 2016. Accessed at https://hbr.org/2011/05/defend-your-research-effective-managers-say-the-same-thing-twice-or-more.
10. Jeffrey A. Hall, "How Many Hours Does It Take to Make a Friend?" *Journal of Social and Personal Relationships* 36, no. 4 (March 15, 2018), pp. 1278–1296. Accessed at https://journals.sagepub.com/doi/full/10.1177/0265407518761225.
11. Adam Hickman and Ilana Ron Levey, "How to Manage Remote Employees," Gallup, August 15, 2019. Accessed at https://www.gallup.com/workplace/263510/manage-remote-employees.aspx; "Flexible Working—An Increasing Trend," International Workplace Group, 2018. Accessed at https://www.iwgplc.com/WorkspaceRevolution/Trends.
12. Ravi S. Gajendran and David A. Harrison, "The Good, the Bad, and the Unknown about Telecommuting: Meta-Analysis of Psychological Mediators and Individual Consequences," *Journal of Applied Psychology* 92, no. 6 (November 2007), pp. 1524–1541. Accessed at https://doi.org/10.1037/0021-9010.92.6.1524.

Chapter 7

1. "Loneliness and the Workplace: 2020 U.S. Report," Cigna Health Corporation, 2020.
2. Caitlin Gallagher, "This Poll Shows What Women and Men Think Is the Most Important Quality in a Partner," HelloGiggles, February 6, 2017. Accessed at https://hellogiggles.com/love-sex/dating/poll-women-men-important-quality-partner/.
3. "Capitalizing on Complexity Insights from the Global Chief Executive Officer Study," IBM Institute for Business Value, May 2010. Accessed at https://www.ibm.com/downloads/cas/1VZV5X8J.
4. James Lichtenberg, Christopher Woock, and Mary Wright, "Ready to Innovate," The Conference Board, 2008. Accessed at https://www.americansforthearts.org/sites/default/files/ReadytoInnovateFull.pdf.
5. Katie Heaney, "Why Do Some People Find It Impossible to Apologize?" The Cut, May 2, 2019. Accessed at https://www.thecut.com/2019/05/why-is-it-so-hard-to-apologize.html.
6. Brown Brené, *Dare to Lead: Brave Work, Tough Conversations, Whole Hearts* (New York: Random House, 2018).
7. Arthur Aron, Edward Melinat, Elaine N. Aron, Robert Darrin Vallone, and Renee J. Bator, "The Experimental Generation of Interpersonal Closeness: A Procedure

and Some Preliminary Findings," *Personality and Social Psychology Bulletin* 23, no. 4 (April 1997), pp. 363–377. Accessed at doi: 10.1177/0146167297234003.

8. Lindsay Mannering, "The Awkward but Essential Art of Office Chitchat," *New York Times*, September 17, 2019. Accessed at https://www.nytimes.com/2019/09/17/style/the-awkward-art-of-office-small-talk.html.

Chapter 9

1. Mitchell Kusy, *Why I Don't Work Here Anymore: A Leader's Guide to Offset the Financial and Emotional Costs of Toxic Employees* (Boca Raton, FL: CRC Press, 2018).
2. Christine Porath and Christine Pearson, "How Toxic Colleagues Corrode Performance," *Harvard Business Review*, August 1, 2014. Accessed at https://hbr.org/2009/04/how-toxic-colleagues-corrode-performance.
3. "Toxic Friends? 8 in 10 People Endure Poisonous Pals," *TODAY*, NBC Universal, August 22, 2011. Accessed at https://www.today.com/health/toxic-friends-8-10-people-endure-poisonous-pals-1C9413205.
4. Mary Kyle, "Impact of Toxic Relationships on Heart Health," EmpowHER, February 25, 2019. Accessed at https://www.empowher.com/heart-disease/content/impact-toxic-relationships-heart-health.
5. Jessica J. Chiang, Naomi I. Eisenberger, Teresa E. Seeman, and Shelley E. Taylor, "Negative and Competitive Social Interactions Are Related to Heightened Proinflammatory Cytokine Activity," *PNAS* 109, no. 6 (February 7, 2012), pp. 1878–1882. Accessed at https://www.pnas.org/content/109/6/1878.

Chapter 10

1. Janice Harper, "The Silence of Shunning: A Conversation with Kipling William," *Psychology Today*, September 4, 2013. Accessed at https://www.psychologytoday.com/us/blog/beyond-bullying/201309/the-silence-shunning-conversation-kipling-william.

Chapter 11

1. "2012 CEO Snapshot Survey," RHR International, 2012. Accessed at https://www.rhrinternational.com/100127/pdf/rs/Snapshot-One-Pager-Statues-ONE.pdf.
2. Nelson, "Friendships in the Workplace Survey."
3. Alex Shaw, Shoham Choshen-Hillel, and Eugene M. Caruso, "Being Biased Against Friends to Appear Unbiased," *Journal of Experimental Social Psychology* 78 (September 2018).

Chapter 12

1. Frank Andrews, *The Art and Practice of Loving* (Los Angeles: Jeremy P. Tarcher, 1992).
2. Travis Bradberry, Jean Greaves, and Patrick Lencioni, *Emotional Intelligence 2.0* (San Diego: TalentSmart, 2009).
3. Daniel B. Kline, "Many Americans Have Had a Work Spouse," *USA Today*, June 11, 2019. Accessed at https://www.usatoday.com/story/money/2019/06/09/work-spouse-can-positive-asset-unless-boundaries-crossed/1371752001/.

4. Stephanie Bucklin, "The 6 Most Common Places Where Affairs Start," Fox News, May 3, 2017. Accessed at https://www.foxnews.com/lifestyle/the-6-most-common-places-where-affairs-start.

Advice for Managers

1. Randall Beck and Jim Harter, "Managers Account for 70% of Variance in Employee Engagement," Gallup.com, August 8, 2019. Accessed at https://news.gallup.com/businessjournal/182792/managers-account-variance-employee-engagement.aspx.
2. "The No. 1 Quality That Makes a Manager Great," Workplace, Gallup, July 11, 2018. Accessed at https://www.gallup.com/workplace/237029/no-quality-makes-manager-great.aspx.
3. Monica Torres, "Survey: 60% of Workers Are Planning Their Exit over Bad Boss," Ladders, October 15, 2018. Accessed at https://www.theladders.com/career-advice/survey-60-of-workers-are-planning-their-exit-over-bad-boss.

www.ingramcontent.com/pod-product-compliance
Lightning Source LLC
LaVergne TN
LVHW032119260325
807038LV00001B/1

* 9 7 8 1 4 0 0 2 1 6 9 9 4 *